BAGEYE AT THE WHEEL

Colin Grant is a historian and BBC radio producer.
He is the author of *Negro with a Hat*, a biography
of Marcus Garvey and *I&I: The Natural Mystics*,
a group biography of the original Wailers, Marley,
Tosh and Livingston. The son of Jamaican emigrants,
he lives in Brighton.

COLIN GRANT

Bageye at the Wheel

A 1970s Childhood in Suburbia

VINTAGE BOOKS
London

Published by Vintage 2013

2 4 6 8 10 9 7 5 3 1

Copyright © Colin Grant 2012

Colin Grant has asserted his right under the Copyright, Designs
and Patents Act 1988 to be identified as the author of this work

First published in Great Britain in 2012 by
Jonathan Cape

Vintage
Random House, 20 Vauxhall Bridge Road,
London SW1V 2SA

www.vintage-books.co.uk

Addresses for companies within The Random House Group Limited
can be found at: www.randomhouse.co.uk/offices.htm

The Random House Group Limited Reg. No. 954009

A CIP catalogue record for this book
is available from the British Library

ISBN 9780099552390

The Random House Group Limited supports The Forest Stewardship
Council® (FSC®), the leading international forest-certification organisation.
Our books carrying the FSC label are printed on FSC®-certified paper.
FSC is the only forest-certification scheme supported by the leading
environmental organisations, including Greenpeace. Our
paper procurement policy can be found at
www.randomhouse.co.uk/environment

Printed and bound in Great Britain by Clays Ltd, St Ives PLC

Farley Hill

THE SLIPPERS SHOULD HAVE BEEN a warning. 'You're no better than me!' Mrs Ayres was screaming at me. She chased after us in her slippers, screaming and squawking. She didn't care that she was scaring my little brother, Baby G, as I pushed him back from the shops on his tricycle. She was blind to him. She raged: 'You're no better than me!' It didn't matter that I hadn't yet reached my eleventh birthday. I was old enough to be told. In fact, it was urgent that I understand. I did understand, didn't I, that I was not superior to her?

I tried to push past her but she grabbed the handlebars. She had heard – it was beyond belief but she had heard people talking – that my mother was plotting to send me to a private school. 'Absurd. Private school? But your mother,' she howled, 'still carries bags to the market. She takes her wet washing to the launderette on the quiet and dries it there, and she's not allowed to dry it there. It's against the law! Only clothes washed at the laundry can be dried there.'

I had always liked Mrs Ayres. When she could afford to – even when she couldn't really manage it – she gave me a little reward for delivering her daily newspapers. 'For the encouragement of others,' she would explain, smiling sweetly and sadly. Pressing the coins back into my palm as I tried to refuse she'd whisper: 'Encouragement sweetens labour.'

Like most of the women on the Farley Hill estate Mrs Ayres was Irish, though she was snooty enough to have been English. There was 'no man around' but Mrs Ayres didn't crave company. She never really associated with her Irish neighbours, and they retaliated by calling her 'Mrs Airs and Graces' behind her back. She had other names, of course. Mostly she was known as the 'General Post Office' (GPO) for the way she gave daily updates on her daughter's progress through teacher training college. If she happened to open the door when you were pushing the newspaper through the letter box, it was a safe bet to ask after her girl. Mrs Ayres would report that her daughter was doing 'splendidly' because she was a 'cut above' the rest of the trainee teachers. The other name for Mrs Ayres – which I'm ashamed to confess I thought of as she bared her angry teeth and blocked the tricycle – was 'Mad Margaret'.

There was always a chance, given that it was close to the time when my father usually came home after the night shift, that Bageye would arrive in the midst of Margaret's madness. Sure enough, at that moment he appeared, stepping off the bus as it pulled up at the stop at the top of the street. It was noticeable that he was wearing his corduroy cap with the peak firmly pulled down shading his eyes – a sign that you should approach with caution. Bageye's shift pattern was never clear. He worked both days and nights but the most dangerous time to be around our father was the hour after a night shift or the hour when he had just woken to begin one. Bageye walked deliberately, but even though he wanted to get to his bed he was not in a hurry. He never did anything in a hurry. I always admired the way my father moved. Bageye walked with the dignity of a footballer on the losing side in an FA Cup final making his way up the steps to collect his runners-up consolation medal.

He looked at the undignified spectacle unfolding outside the shops and slowed his pace. For a moment I imagined he would intervene and free us from Mrs Ayres's grip. But though he slowed he did not stop. He kept on walking until he disappeared into Castlecroft Road. I should not have been surprised. Bageye was not a man for street scenes.

Baby G and I only had to endure a few more minutes before Mrs Ayres was all punched out. She spluttered a few more words, and that was that. She may have been mad but she wasn't mad-mad: she was more sober-mad. Drunk on the madness for a while, she would sober up and regret it soon after. Most of the time she was quite sensible really. Mrs Ayres stepped to one side. She looked exhausted. We were free to go but it would have been rude just to leave her there without saying anything.

'Any news?' I asked about her daughter. Mrs Ayres smiled weakly, reached into her purse, counted out a few coins and handed them to me, saying: 'It's not much but you'll need all you can get now, won't you, dear, what with the fees and everything.'

The private school news had leaked out even though nothing had been decided. Mum had mentioned it as an idea (nothing more) in passing the previous week and Bageye had paid no attention. In fact, he had muttered something like: 'Stop talk tripe, woman.' Yet now Mrs Ayres was screaming about it all over the estate as if it was a reality. Bageye probably hadn't heard the news, but I was in no hurry to get back.

Even though I delayed our return, pushing Baby G around the block a few times, there were worrying signs, when we reached the house on Castlecroft Road, that Bageye was still awake. His bedroom curtains had not been closed and from the front door you could smell the ackee and salt fish frying in the pan. Bageye sat at the kitchen table scanning the racing pages while Mum stood over him serving his breakfast with a heavy hand. The clanking of the metal serving spoon on the plate as Blossom dished out his food made me wince and wish I'd gone round to the back door.

I hadn't worked out that statistically it made no sense trying to hide things from our father because he invariably found out. I began going through a list of possible explanations for the altercation with Mad Margaret that included a fire alarm and minor earthquake, and soon realised that it was the same list I'd rolled out the last time questions were asked by my father about my involvement in some low-class back-a-yard affair. If I'd thought about it more deeply I might have come to the conclusion that it was *always* the same list. But before I reached the 'sighting of UFOs' justification, Bageye asked: 'Wha'appen in the street with the Ayres woman – wha'gwan there?'

'Something about private school,' I said, trying to sound casual, but it came out with the confidence of someone who realised they had just stepped in warm dog shit. Bageye chewed on the food without pleasure. The mouthfuls of ackee and salt fish were just something to get through without spoiling his real appetite for a smoke afterwards.

'In the house?' he barked, pointing his knife at the tricycle. 'You nah know you don't suppose for have that t'ing in the house? Cho, man, is no wonder the lino brock up so.'

Bageye started to twitch the way he did when the dark mood took him. It wasn't exactly his fault, I'd worked out: it was just the mood. You could trace the mood working its way into his chest and taking possession of him. Blossom stopped what she was doing at the stove and backed away from it with slow and deliberate steps, all the while keeping an eye on Bageye the way gunslingers did in the movies. It was funny but not in a way that made you want to laugh. She dried her hands on the apron and picked up some kind of pamphlet. It might as well have been a gun. Immediately, I grasped the meaning of Mad Margaret's outburst. The pamphlet was a school brochure. *St Columba's College* was emblazoned in italics boldly across the cover.

Blossom walked up to Bageye and slid the brochure across the kitchen table. I took the chance to push Baby G on the tricycle quietly across the kitchen floor and out the back door, shutting it gently behind us. Baby G pedalled down the garden path and I followed.

Even from the end of the garden you could hear the explosion of voices in the kitchen. It took about ten minutes for the shouting to die down and for me to summon the courage to return. Blossom was back in position at the stove humming a sad hymn. Bageye was gone, departed for his bed. The brochure was missing too.

At Mrs Knight's

THE CAR PLANT WAS MORE than a mile away but if you closed your eyes, as I did, and listened carefully that Thursday afternoon, you could just about make out the eerie factory horn at Vauxhall Motors signalling the end of a shift. You might even hear the chatter of excited voices carried on the wind as the men, still in their overalls, streamed out from the factory, lighting up a well-deserved cigarette, and headed towards the Portakabin where clerks handed out their wages.

I held that picture in my head until, thankfully, the starlings took it away. They came crashing in overhead and onto the recreation ground, forcing my eyes open. I tried to count all the birds in the flock before the giant tail turned into a head, the head into wings, and then flew north. The perimeter of the rec was bordered by a huge metal fence separating it from the motorway and for a short while the flock raced the motor cars. It occurred to me that the drivers must have been workers from Vauxhall's. The individual cars were too many to count, and I ended up counting all the imagined workers at the Portakabin instead, separating them into the ones who got on their bikes and the ones lucky enough to get into cars. And that was my mistake. It let in the first thoughts of my father. Until then I'd managed to keep him out. But most of the cyclists at Vauxhall's, like the neighbour across the road, wore caps. My father wore a cap.

Obviously, though he did not drive a car, he would never have mounted a bicycle. A man like my father could hardly have travelled from Jamaica to begin a new life in England only to end up, like a deadbeat, riding a bicycle. No, sir, a bike did not become a man. A cap, though, was another matter. Even so I couldn't remember him wearing a cap when he'd left for work this morning. Thoughts jumbled together into a mighty mess. I half closed my eyes and ran, holding my breath.

In my mind, I conjured the starlings again, a monotonous procession of new Vauxhall cars pounding off the production line, an army of bell-ringing cyclists and finally Eddy Merckx, in a tight yellow jersey, on the last stage of the Tour de France − all chased me to the finishing tape at 42 Castlecroft Road; and before I got to thirty seconds of breathlessness I was home. But by the time I closed the front door a thread of thought about the cap still remained. I don't know why I was panicking about the cap. It was stupid really. Even before changing into my house clothes, I found myself rifling through the coats on the rack and then tiptoeing into my parents' bedroom to check the back of the cupboard door. My father's golden brown corduroy cap was missing. Was that a good sign? It surprised me that I'd never considered before that the hats he routinely wore might be indicative of his mood or be set aside for specific occasions: he was, after all, a hat man.

'The pickney can be dead for hungry,' our mum would often complain, 'and that man g'wan buy

himself another hat. And don't bother tell him any
different, you know. The man have more hat than
John dream.' I couldn't have told you how many
visions or dreams John the Baptist had had but it was
certainly true that Bageye had more hats than his spar
Tidy Boots had shoes, and Tidy Boots had a lot of
shoes – perhaps a dozen pairs. My father – all the
fellas called him Bageye – was as known for his hats
as he was for the permanent bags under his eyes.

I had heard it said that if you wanted to know
something about a man you should look at his feet.
But with Bageye, his head was a better place to start.
Now that the cap was firmly established on my father's
head, it was a struggle to picture him without a hat,
though he would have been critical of any man who
wore one indoors.

The thought was so intense it was almost audible.
But it wasn't. In fact, there was an absence of sound;
even the drone of the factory horn had died away. I
tore off my school uniform, beating my all-time record,
for I was beginning to suspect that I hadn't really
heard that factory horn but had tricked myself into
thinking I had more time to get out of the house
and down to the rec's playing fields before my father
returned. As it was, Bageye was likely to be only
minutes away.

Thursday was the very best day in the week for
our father: pay day. In the last hour he'd have picked
up the crisp brown envelope with its bundle of
banknotes and a few coins. Thursdays presented us
with both danger and opportunity. If you were around
when Bageye got back and his good mood still held
then you might find some of those coins gifted to

you, but if it was the other, more usual, blacker mood that took him then, my friend, you were done for – trapped for the duration of the fierce negotiations that would ensue between Bageye and Mum over the amount of house money to come out of the 'one wage'. You had to go home from school to change and you couldn't always get the timing right. It was a gamble. You'd get an early warning about whether or not you'd made a mistake by the sound Bageye's key made turning in the front door. But by then it would be too late.

Mum was in the bathroom on her knees beside the bath, wringing out the water, with her bare hands, from the giant snake of wet sheets and blankets that she'd washed and rinsed earlier. It was heavy and relentless work. Laundry occupied the bath more often than my parents and us children. Bageye's house-money calculations might stretch to the sixpences for the dryers at the launderette but never to the expense of washing the clothes in the machines, just as Mad Margaret suspected.

Every week Blossom would have to wrestle with the sheets. Many would have forgiven our mother for imagining that her hands gripped our father's neck when she wrung out the sheets. She was not shy of voicing Bageye's shortcomings as a husband. 'He actually have me like a servant gal,' was her constant cry. Blossom resented him for the coarsening of her hands which for the first nineteen years of her life (before they'd met) had been shaped for more delicate tasks; she blamed him for the building up of biceps on arms that had once been destined to remain slim and ladylike, and to draw the flattery of admirers. I shouted my hellos but didn't pop my head round the bathroom door. I never liked to witness her on her knees, except in prayer.

At about 5.30 p.m. my father's key was thrust forcibly into the lock. The sound filled me with dread. Strangely though, once he was in, the front door closed more gently than expected – the way it might if one of us kids had come back home later than he'd agreed. Bageye had his back to me. He spun round abruptly and caught me staring at him. I focused immediately on my shoes. It was one mistake after another as I sensed his eyes also travelling down to my feet, to the shoes, scuffed and caked in dried mud.

'I don't have any football boots,' I explained. 'Teacher made me play in my shoes.'

'Which teacher?'

'PE teacher.'

'Him nah have name?'

No matter how hard I tried I couldn't find the teacher's name in the black hole of my mind. I couldn't even remember the name of my school, or how many heel-to-toe steps it took to get to school, and I had only counted them this morning. A single tear slipped out and slid down my cheek, which was odd because I didn't particularly feel like crying. My father pretended not to notice. What's more, he seemed more distracted by the large paper bag he'd brought home. The bag was sealed at the top and you got the impression that he was guarding whatever was inside. He was reluctant to put it down but needed to get something out of his pockets. He shifted the weight, balancing the bag awkwardly in one hand,

and with his free hand reached into a pocket and took out a small bag of sweets.

'Well, you cyaan' play barefoot. Not in this ah country. But you should-a play in goal.' He tossed the sweets bag to me. It was full of toffee nuts.

'Don't finish them one time. Leave some for your brother and sister.'

You see, this is where you had to be so careful with our father. Ordinarily you might have assumed that he resented us, but every so often he did something to cast doubt on that fact.

Bageye started to climb the staircase just as Blossom was coming down. They greeted each other neutrally, like two unfriendly tenants forced to be civil by their unfortunate proximity. When Blossom reached the bottom, she held onto the banister for a moment. She was weary from the washing but some old instinct drove her on. She turned and followed her husband up the stairs. It wasn't long before her voice began to change.

Blossom sounded as if her arms were folded tightly across her chest. Her discussion points were met by Bageye's low, growly tone: a series of warning 'harrumphs' which grew louder as Blossom strove to make her point. My father was a man who didn't like people to know his business. Mum wasn't too fond either of the gossip-mongers, the 'carry go/bring come' traders in tittle-tattle. But where she took exception to Bageye's tendency towards secrecy was when that attitude extended to his wife. From the bottom of the stairs I crept slowly upwards one step at a time. The discussion inevitably was over money.

'Hold five pound for now,' Bageye suggested.

'Five! That cyann' even feed one mouth.'

'Wha'appen to last week money?' asked Bageye drolly.

'Me still waiting for last week money.'

'But me nah give you ten last week? The ten finish already? Why you cyann' manage yourself better?'

'Is wha'appen?' Blossom snapped back. 'You gamble out the money already?'

Back and forth they went. In their argument my mum was the consistently buzzing bee. My father was the man who only after a long while notices that the bee is in the room, and takes an occasional swing at it; when that doesn't work he reaches for a newspaper which is rolled up to swat the bloody thing; and finally he removes a shoe and chases the tormenting bee around the room, hoping it will settle on a wall long enough for him to smash it with the heel.

Actually, now that he was anchored in the middle of the room, occupied with ironing his shirt on the ironing board, Bageye chased with his voice, and he let his wife know that he was not going to scorch his shirt on account of her. The shirt was too important for that. It had cost him a few penny; he wasn't saying how much but it was enough. The iron clanked on the creaking board; starch was liberally applied to cuffs and collar, while Blossom laid before her husband an inventory of all of the costs to be met by the house money – not luxuries but bare necessities.

By way of illustration she explained. 'Spring on the pickney mattress a-come through. The mattress want change. Should-a t'row away long time.' But her immediate concern was the toilet: 'Toilet block. No more newspaper cyann' flush. It block, it block.'

Bageye answered that he still had the pardner money to pay Mrs Knight. If there was 'one money' that needed to be paid, that couldn't be deferred, it was the pardner money – Mrs Knight's unofficial savings and banking system that many, if not all, of Bageye's fellow Jamaicans paid into. The pardner money was sacrosanct. It was an investment. It was our future.

'Yes, but while the grass is growing,' said Mum, 'the horse is starving.'

But Bageye turned the argument, and started to sound like his wife, talking of sacrifices and necessary evils. It couldn't be helped and after settling with Mrs Knight there would be little left from the 'one wage'.

'Stop talk tripe, man, the pay cyann' finish, you just get pay.'

Bageye finished ironing the shirt. He held it up to the light for inspection. He was pleased with the result. 'Come, we go talk it out.' Although he still sounded as if he was bartering, he was at least gentlemanly about it.

'Is wha' you need? You can manage with ten, for now?'

Mum snorted at the suggestion: 'You must be joke!'

I'd reached the landing and could hear everything apart from the occasional dropout. Despite the growing conciliatory tone, the lull in the conversation was worrying. At these times, if you listened carefully you could work out a pattern in what was said: essentially, it was a game of high-risk bluff. No matter the escalation in the quarrel, Bageye and Blossom mostly abided by an unwritten and unspoken code that limited the nature of hostilities – a kind of equivalent to our rule as kids that when shaping up for a fight no kicking or scratching was allowed. Even so our parents' arguments had changed in recent months, and were liable to take a sudden, unexpected and nasty turn. Then rules of engagement would be abandoned; a demon would take over Bageye's soul, forcing him to pull out all the drawers on the kitchen unit so that the cutlery cascaded to the floor; to take scissors to the leaves of any plant left alive; to upturn boiling pans of water on the stove; or to yank the toilet chain till it came away from the cistern. It was best to be prepared for escape to a safe distance beyond range of Bageye's bomb blast.

From the top landing, I leapt with arms outstretched; one hand grasped the banister, the other pressed into the wall. I swung and flew down to the final step, like Olga Korbut in the Olympics. Feet together, knees together, arms up and out, straight in the air for a perfect 10.

On the crawl back up to the top, I saw Mum coming out of the bedroom. She crossed the landing and went into the bathroom. She tried the toilet. There was a slight groan from the cistern but it did not flush. She did not try a second time. A few minutes passed. In the silence I imagined tears but all you could really hear was the slap of washing on the side of the bath, and a sad hymn on her trembling lips. Eventually, Blossom emerged carrying a laundry basket filled to the brim with steaming sheets and blankets. I did my invisible trick, flattening myself against the wall.

'I see you, you know,' she whispered. Remarkably, there was a half-smile in her voice as she trudged down the steps.

I peeled myself from the wall and tried to peer through the crack in the door to their bedroom. Bageye looked as though he was checking the paper bag that he'd brought home. Through the slit I saw, or thought I saw, the head of a doll in that bag. I only caught sight of it briefly because Bageye slid the bag inside the wardrobe. There was something about the way he gently pushed the door closed that made you think that you'd witnessed an act you ought not to have seen. Odder still was the doll itself. Toys and toyshops never registered on our father's radar. If he'd bought presents in the past, it was only under pressure from Joe Burns who'd once mysteriously acquired a vanload of spinning tops that he needed to shift quickly and accepted ridiculous – 'might as well be giving it away' – money. Even so, Shirleen's birthday was still a month away.

Bageye resumed his meticulous ironing. The clank of the iron on the board had a happier ring to it than before. He took his sweet time, giving as much attention to his handkerchief as his wife, speed-ironing, would have allowed for one of our shirts or pairs of trousers. There was a snap to his movements that perfectly complemented the sharp creases on the sleeves of his shirt and starched stiffness of collar and cuffs. The shirt brought out even more fully the straightness of his back and shoulders. He rolled up the metal spring armbands on his sleeves, slipped on a jacket, and eased the handkerchief into the awaiting breast pocket. Finally, he applied a dash of mouth spray – just one spray, not too heavy – and checked himself in the wardrobe mirror. Even to my eye the end result was as satisfying as the final piece of the

16

jigsaw slotted into the puzzle. All that was needed now was to crack open the playing cards; turn the chicken; put on a record and break the seal on the bottle of rum: Bageye was ready for a night of poker at Mrs Knight's. His wife would not be accompanying him. Bageye bounded out of the house before Blossom's return with the empty basket for the next load of laundry, having hung out so many blankets on the line that it sagged and threatened to snap. Only the wardrobe mirror and I witnessed the Thursday-afternoon transformation.

The scent of aftershave and mouth spray remained in the bedroom after Bageye's departure. But now that he'd left – and ahead of my brother and sisters coming home from school – I could check up on the secret of Shirleen's present that he had stashed in the wardrobe. It was a delicious secret that only I was party to. I'd be able to hint at it and frustrate and annoy everyone else when they pressed for details – as they surely would. However, when I looked inside the wardrobe, it was nowhere to be found. Bageye must have anticipated its discovery and found a more secure hiding place for it. And this was always worth remembering about our father because it was rarely revealed: despite everything, he was capable of surprises.

Mrs Knight had a big semi-detached corner house on Hazelbury Crescent. Though being close to Bury Park and the Luton football ground wasn't ideal, the house was located in a tiny upmarket residential enclave – 'down them parts where money people live' as Blossom would say. Even the word 'crescent' had an exclusive ring to it. Black people didn't tend to live on crescents. Our mother wasn't the only one impressed by Mrs Knight. Plenty of people remarked that she had her 'head screwed on'. Particularly as, if you didn't know her, you might have thought that she was no better off than anybody else. If, for instance, Boasty Morgan had lived on Hazelbury Crescent, then the whole world would have known about it, but Mrs Knight was not 'a talkative'.

Most days Blossom was full of admiration for Mrs Knight's shrewdness: 'Don't you worry, she have two penny.' But the Lord divides. Mrs Knight was blessed when it came to money but she hadn't been too lucky in the looks department. Left on its own, a comb would have had difficulty passing through her coarse, natty hair. Mrs Knight relied on Vaseline and a hot copper comb to straighten it. She wasn't a great beauty or even pretty but she wasn't ugly either. That must have been some consolation. 'Tree nah grow in her face,' other women said about her, almost as a compliment.

Bageye and the fellas couldn't keep away from Mrs Knight's; our mother would whisper to us, almost as a warning not to follow them, that only a certain kind of man went there: the man who wanted to gamble. Then, in our mother's telling, Mrs Knight took on a far more sinister demeanour. She became a great bird of prey – one with sharp talons which, if they ever dug into you, you'd never wriggle free from. There'd be no more hope because 'she gone with you'.

All of us children listened closely to Blossom's tales

of the goings-on at Mrs Knight's because each one of us knew that at some stage, no matter how reluctantly, our mother would be forced to send us there. Looked at another way, the stories were actually military briefings in preparation for operation 'Extract Money from Bageye at Mrs Knight's'.

On a Thursday night, Mum informed us, 55 Hazelbury Crescent became a gambling den, 'a bull party'. 'Jus' a few men drinking rum, no gal, jus' rum there.' Of all the bulls at the party, there was no mistaking our mother's assessment that Bageye was the most foolish. Bageye just loved being there. He'd get to Mrs Knight's early, ahead of everybody else, and help stoke the fire and prepare the drinks. Mum groaned at the thought: 'When the game start, him is the chargehand. Though what him in charge of, God is for tell.' In theory the chargehand was responsible for the poker table; he ensured that the gambling went smoothly and that there was no cheating. But it wasn't a paid position, as far as Mum could tell. 'Mrs Knight there a-use the man. Yes, bwoy, if you want jackass for ride, here comes Bageye.'

The men started to assemble round about dinnertime. For the majority, just like Bageye, it was a dress-up occasion. The current line-up at Mrs Knight's included Shine, Tidy Boots, Pumpkin Head, Scandal, Soon Come, Big Roy and Summer Wear. Each man was reduced to that which was most obvious about him. Some were luckier than others. 'Shine', of course, was bald; 'Tidy Boots' was fastidious. 'Bageye' had baggy eyes. Everyone's favourite was 'Summer Wear', so called because he had come to this country in a light summer suit and continued to wear suits, preferably linen ones, no matter the weather; he refused to wear heavy winter clothes.

Apart from Joe Burns, we never knew their surnames. The fellas never gave out their real names because you never knew what could be done with them. If you made an enemy of someone and they knew your name, well, they could take it and write it down and put the paper with your name on it in the heel of their shoe. It never made much sense to us kids, but a lot of the big people seemed to believe in it, and grew suspicious if ever you made the mistake of asking them what they were really called. When we pressed our mother for an explanation she said it was 'only the lower class of people' that dealt in such foolishness. But if you weren't sure, you didn't take chances. Everyone remembered how Castus used to laugh about the silly superstitions of the backward people – the 'nasty Naygars' he called them – until that time when there was a brief mix-up over the payslips and one of the men picked up Castus's wage packet by mistake even though his name was on it. Castus wasn't worried about anyone learning how much he earned, but he was extremely anxious that his name had been revealed. And that same night, though Castus was the most skilled poker player, he lost the most money he'd ever lost at Mrs Knight's. And according to Mum, from that day on, Castus hadn't been seen at the poker game.

Alongside Bageye, Pioneer was the most constant presence at Hazelbury Crescent. Pioneer beat all comers with his snazzy dress sense. He was a generation older than Bageye and the rest, and a regular at Mrs Knight's from the very beginning. They called him

Pioneer not because he came over on the *Windrush* ten years before most others, but rather because of his obsession with a certain brand of hi-fi. He had peculiar taste. Despite being a Jamaican, and, by his reckoning, a deep, deep countryman, he was not too fond of reggae. Pioneer wouldn't allow 'no damn monkey music 'pon the machine'. That machine was only built for African hi-life. Pure hi-life morning till night.

He was a man of contrasts. You could even see it in his face: from the heavy, demonic eyebrows to the kind of pencil-thin moustache that would have once lined the upper lip of some silent-screen Hollywood rascal. He was an old guy, long in the saddle, and took his place, by rights, at the head of the table; he was always the first to deal. This was only after a set of rituals from which he never departed. Before snapping open the pack, Pioneer would retire to the bathroom to brush his teeth. Then he'd pull up a chair at the poker table and hold out an empty glass for his first whisky of the night, on the strict understanding that it was poured from a new bottle.

'Never drink from a bottle if the seal break,' he would warn, 'and never eat fruit if it have stone.' Occasionally someone new to the scene would question the wisdom of the older man's pronouncements, causing a flicker of conspiratorial glances round the table as they anticipated Pioneer's response.

The new boy would be mercilessly rounded on and despatched with: 'Listen, likkle bwoy, I been here from time. And . . .' here Pioneer would pause, it seemed, for ever, '. . . the Englishman was fine with

21

me until . . .' and at this point his arms would fan out over the room at all the fellas propped up nursing their beers, 'until all you Negroes came over and messed things up'.

Pioneer lived up in Ipswich but every Thursday made the trek to Luton and the poker game. It was rumoured that he kept not only a pink budgerigar, but also a woman, an Englishwoman – some even said she was his wife – hidden away up there. It could not have been true because Pioneer was always adamant that his woman was as fine as any African queen, and that 'as long as me deh 'pon dis eart' me nah check no pork'. It was the kind of thing that every man said of the dangerous white women in town. Only Joe Burns unashamedly carried on with them. At least, that was the common belief of the fellas' wives. It wasn't long, though, before the rumour began to circulate about some of the 'loose Irish gal' and the stockingless, 'bluefoot' Englishwomen making their way to Mrs Knight's at the weekend to entice the men with their dirty dancing. Mum, though, held onto the belief that Bageye and his spars would never sink so low. Perhaps she needed to maintain that fiction. Otherwise, it would have been doubly difficult to countenance sending her children down to Hazelbury Crescent.

In the TV show *Mission Impossible* the agents were always given the option of declining the mission. Mum could afford us no such luxury. The £10 would not even touch the surface of the household needs. The toilet would remain blocked if we continued to force scraps of newspaper into the bowl. Toilet paper would make it onto the shopping list, Mum advised, but we had to go easy with it. The mattress was more problematic. It had been turned so many times we had lost count. Not a night seemed to pass without another lethally sharp spring shooting through the canvas. Push one spring back and another would pop up elsewhere. A replacement mattress was the only practical solution but there was little that she could do about it for now.

A visit to Blundell's was impossible as we had already exceeded the credit limit at that department store. And yes, Blossom had started a secret mattress fund but it hadn't yet reached halfway. Whenever it did creep towards the winning figure an emergency would arise, requiring Blossom to dip into it. The last time Blossom had dragged herself to Hazelbury Crescent, Bageye had fumed at the outrage: he'd kept his seat at the table and just looked at her all evening with his dry eye and never said a word. Blossom had returned empty-handed except for a bag of sugar from one of the tenants at Mrs Knight's who had taken pity on her.

Our mother had her pride, but she would go there again. Of course she would go to Mrs Knight's herself, it was just that there was a greater chance of success, of Bageye being shamed into improving on the £10, if a couple of his pickney stood by the poker table when the cards were being dealt.

The house was a fortress, set back from the road and hidden from prying eyes by a slatted wooden fence on one side and by a hedge that was double my height on the other. Though never breached by strangers, its neat borders were mocked by empty beer cans shoved into the hedge – left as calling cards by old drunkards en route from the nearby off-licence. Thoughtless perhaps, but Bageye believed otherwise. One of his repeated lessons to us was that, unlike the American who would tell the black man to his face he didn't like him and that he was not wanted, the Englishman preferred to leave a message. Nevertheless, despite the nightly acts of spite, these unwanted decorations never multiplied as each of the fellas – when they dropped by Mrs Knight's yard – made it their business to remove at least one can and place it in the bin round the side of the house before making an entrance.

Selma and I had been sent on the mission to Mrs Knight's. I couldn't reach any of the empty Heinekens in the hedge and, even though I explained that it was bad form not to remove a can, Selma, who was four years older than me, refused outright to climb onto my shoulders. She also made plain that the way I was increasingly trying to imitate how the fellas behaved – and worse still, how they spoke – was faintly ridiculous and extremely irritating. Furthermore, she declined to knock on the front door, insisting it was my turn.

Mrs Knight's husband – they simply called him Knight – opened the door. He looked down at us from his great height, pulling the cord on his dressing gown so tight that the material squeaked. Knight was rarely out of that robe. He was a man who liked his bed. Bageye called him the laziest man he had ever met, but whenever Knight grew irritable his wife would tell him: 'You're overdoing it, man, go back to sleep.' Everything he did was exaggerated. His yawn was wide enough to turn his face inside out. It went on for some little while. Like his wife he was not a talkative person, but even more wilfully so. Over time, Knight had disciplined himself to use only a set number of phrases. He must have been low on stock because, at first, he declined to say anything at all. Instead he gestured with his hands, turning them palm up. Had it been his shoulders you'd have called it a shrug – a way of asking what we wanted without the bother of actually speaking.

From somewhere at the back of the house his wife shouted: 'Ah who dat now?'

'Look like Bageye son,' answered Knight eventually. It wasn't clear whether he was being extra ignorant or just acting as big people often did, talking about us as if we were deaf.

'Is Bageye son that?'

Mrs Knight's curiosity was not matched by her husband. 'It look so,' he said, and standing to one side muttered, 'Come, you a-let in all the cold air, man.'

He closed the front door behind us and climbed the stairs two at a time, entering the first room off the landing. We waited for Knight to come out again but he never showed. He must have gone back to bed.

There was a funereal stillness about the hallway that couldn't be explained by the hour – that dead time between the afternoon and evening. Every so often the quiet was broken by murmuring voices in various distant parts of the building. They seemed to meet in the hallway, swirl around us and depart again. Strips of light could be seen at the bottoms of the doors off the hallway, but otherwise it was as long and dark as a tunnel. All the doors were firmly closed. Then the end door was suddenly pulled ajar. I reached for Selma's hand. She did not resist. We only saw the outline of a female figure. For a big person she seemed tiny.

'Do you want to see my doll's house?' she asked.

We knew about Mrs Knight's daughter but had never met her. In fact, we'd often overheard our parents talking about her: how she was going to private school for 'a little bit of polish'. She still had on her school uniform and it was surprising that it didn't seem any posher than ours. As she came closer you could see what people meant when they said 'that's no jacket' when describing her: she couldn't have been more than seven or eight but she looked just like a mini version of Mrs Knight.

'Do you want to?' she asked again, sounding as you were supposed to if you had plums in your mouth.

'I'm afraid we've no time,' Selma answered. 'We're here on official business.' I didn't exactly appreciate Selma's snooty attitude to the Knight girl: she was only half my sister's age, after all. But Selma was moving on. She extracted her hand from my grip – overdoing it really, as if she were freeing herself from some wrestling hold. Trying the nearest door, she pushed it open and gestured to me to follow her.

It turned out to be a kind of dining room, kitted out with random bits of furniture. An oval dining table filled almost the entire space. The rest of the room was taken up with non-matching chairs, a gramophone and a couple of bedroom dressing tables which functioned as cabinets for crockery. Jesus and Mary competed as usual for wall space in heavy

26

gold-plated frames, and there was a mishmash of other decorations, some of which were actually quite nice. My favourite was the wall rug depicting cartoon dogs wearing pork-pie hats and playing snooker. We wandered into the next room, and it was similar but not the same. I guess you'd say both were functional, not places where Mrs Knight herself would relax. They would do as meeting rooms for the shifting number of tenants she had dotted around the house. In fact, the rooms seemed to have been furnished entirely from Bernard's bargain store. Mrs Knight would have got a good rent for them. She was born to haggle.

Judging from the few times she'd been to Castlecroft Road when Bageye had come up short on the hand for his pardner money, her approach was direct and effective. Mrs Knight would simply say: 'But you must can do better than that,' repeating it over and over, but not in a scolding way – more like a stern but favourite teacher whom you didn't want to disappoint by letting yourself down – until she got the answer she wanted.

We heard her before we saw her and it was always a shock to experience that rich and spicy, but ultimately commanding voice, coming out of such a tiny frame. Even a suggestion that the chicken be taken out of the oven sounded like a command of the utmost importance, and your subsequent obedience to it the most vital life decision you were likely ever to make. She was the womanly equivalent of a beanie man. Tough? Mrs Knight was a conker soaked for generations in brine and baked slowly over decades. True, she was starting to look a little preserved, wind-dried rather than salted, but she still managed to keep all the bulls at the rum party in the paddock.

The garage-like extension to her kitchen served as this particular paddock, and the fellas who'd lived all their youths under the Caribbean sun and moon loved it for its semblance of home, for its indoor/outdoor feel. In all of Luton it could not have been bettered. You couldn't really fault Bageye for making it his second home.

We'd only been to that part of the house once before, and neither of us could remember how to get there. We stumbled blindly along, hoping for further signs of life. No words passed between us, and though she would never have admitted it, I could tell from the unusually tentative way she walked that Selma was just as nervous as me of being caught somewhere that might have been deemed out of bounds. There was the added complication that we hadn't worked out what we'd say when we eventually came face to face with our father. The voice trail didn't immediately lead to Mrs Knight. There was a maze of rooms that had to be discreetly explored before we discovered a false door, which at first we'd mistaken for the continuation of a wall, that took us to the kitchen.

Even though we'd been anticipating it we were still taken aback by the distinctive sound of Bageye. He sat at the poker table dealing the cards. Actually, the dealing was interrupted because every time he dealt a card to Uncle Darcus – whom the men (unbeknownst to him) had recently started to call 'Scandal' – there was a commotion as Scandal pushed the card back to him.

'I'm out. I'm out,' Scandal kept repeating.

'But you cyann' jus' come clear the pot and gone,' answered Bageye. 'You must give we a chance to win back the money.' Bageye was near the outer edges of his temper. Mrs Knight stood behind him. She leant down and whispered something to Bageye and then left by another door.

It didn't take long to work out what was going on. As was his way, as soon as Scandal had won his first hand, he'd become determined to sit out the rest of the game. Ignoring the protests, Scandal stood up, pocketed his money and moved away from the table. His place was immediately taken by Monty, who'd been itching to get into the game. There was a collective groan as he sat down, and an exchange of pained glances between the other players. What distinguished Monty from all of the other fellas was a single fingernail. Monty had let the monster nail grow to twice the length of any other nail. It was generally assumed that he was using that nail to mark the cards, though no one was ever brave enough to call him on it. Instead, at various stages of the evening the conversation would turn to nail varnish, manicures, even emery boards. Failing to provoke a response, a man would ask another whether he had any nail clippers he might borrow; or Monty's neighbour at the poker table would open his wallet and a pair of nail scissors might drop accidentally onto the table. But Monty never noticed – or more likely chose not to notice – any of these antics; and his run of good luck at poker continued unabated.

It was Monty who first spotted us. Drily, he suggested that we pull up a chair, as the game hadn't started yet, and there was room for one or two more.

Neither of us moved. Bageye lifted his head briefly, so briefly that you might not have noticed. It was his way of acknowledging his progeny, and putting us on notice that he would be sorting us out later on: I didn't care to speculate what he might have in store for us. Monty wasn't finished with us yet.

'But you have money? You must have money to sit at this ah table. If you don't have money, you must have collateral.' When we still didn't answer he attempted to draw the others into the fun.

'Is Bageye son that? Who know? How about you, Bageye, you recognise the pickney? Dem is with you?'

The world would come to an end before Bageye answered. But having started down this path, Monty had no choice but to continue.

'Bwoy, Bageye start him pickney young though.'

'Nah must,' answered Scandal. 'Nah blood follow vein?'

Bageye paid no attention to Monty or to his cousin's intervention. He split the cards in two and began shuffling distractedly. 'Slow motion' does not do justice to the pace: it would have been impossible to have shuffled them any slower. Monty sat opposite but Bageye seemed to stare through and beyond Monty to where Summer Wear was perched on a crate by the back door.

'I'm sitting here and I'm thinking,' said Bageye, so quietly that he captured everyone's attention. 'I'm sitting here and I'm thinking . . . I'm thinking: *What is wrong with Summer Wear?*'

Every single man turned towards Summer Wear. As was his way, Summer Wear had dressed in a thin summer suit, though it was cold outside and not much warmer in the extended kitchen. No one was too surprised to see that he was shivering. But Summer Wear was also sweating. His hair was dank, and his skin was pasty and the colour of putty. The men stared hard at him, unable to speak, and the power of their collective gaze seemed to cause him to rise up from the crate. Almost immediately Summer Wear doubled over and vomited.

Bageye vaulted over to Summer Wear and caught him before he fell. Everyone looked horrified. Tidy Boots, in particular, looked as if he might cry, but then he simply muttered: 'Ten-pound shoes.' Tidy Boots had not been quick enough to move his feet. Though only specks of vomit had spattered his shoes, it was enough to cause him distress.

'Ten-pound shoes. Damn. Ten-pound shoes!'

Bageye told him to stop being an arse. 'This is not a joke-joke t'ing, you know, super. Give me your keys.' Bageye was set on driving Summer Wear to hospital. A discussion broke out over the wisdom of such a move because everyone knew the Luton and Dunstable Hospital's reputation for experimenting on black people in the name of medical research. If it was the L&D, Monty suggested: 'Forget the ambulance, you might as well send a hearse.' But then someone reminded the group that there was a black sister in charge of one of the wards, and she was not likely to let one of her kinsmen die.

Tidy Boots surrendered his car keys, and it was warming to see how Bageye took charge, directing two of the fellas to prop up Summer Wear and guide him to the car. He'd follow, once he'd counted the pot. After all, he was still the 'chargehand' and everyone, eyeing their share of the pot, agreed that it was best to be practical. Yes, it was an emergency, but there was no emergency that couldn't wait.

As Bageye counted the notes, Selma strode up to the table. She had a message from our mother.

'It cyann' wait?' Bageye said.

'No. She says to tell you the ten is not enough.'

'Well, she have for hold the ten for now.'

'But she says: "While the grass is growing, the horse is starving."'

Bageye looked well and truly vexed. 'Monty, man, you can break a ten for me?' he asked. Monty gave him two £5 notes in exchange for the £10, and holding up a £5 note, Bageye addressed me and my sister: 'Which one of you is the bad man?' He didn't wait for an answer; just folded up the £5, slapped it into my palm and exited in a hurry out the back door.

While the men debated who was going to clean up Summer Wear's mess on the floor and whether someone should fetch Mrs Knight, Selma and I slipped out of the kitchen, back the way we had come. She was giggly and so was I. Despite everything we had triumphed: mission accomplished, and on top of which it was hard to deny a smidgen of pride in the way our father had acted: he'd done the right thing, not just by Summer Wear but by his family, however reluctantly, as well.

After a few minutes the old unspoken rancour between us returned. We couldn't quite manage to retrace our steps. If I was to blame, then so was she. Somehow we found ourselves in the room of the little girl. She was sitting in front of her doll's house. Selma tugged at me not to dally but I felt as if my feet were glued to the floor. Propped up in a toy chair beside Mrs Knight's daughter was a doll, a brand new doll. It looked very, very familiar.

'You came back,' said the girl with the sweetest of smiles.

The Itch

'MY HAND ITCH ME,' SAID Mum, scratching the palm of one hand with the fingers of the other. 'I wonder who gwan give me money?' She said it out loud but really she was talking to herself. If you didn't know any better, you'd have believed that the idea was somehow novel and strange to her, but we'd heard her speak in this way on many occasions. We went about our business and paid her no mind.

The itching carried on all morning. Though she was as rough with her hand as she might have been with a persistently irritating child, she didn't appear to be troubled by it; just the opposite. She sang a hymn softly as she worked the dustpan and brush in the corners of the living room. If there was not quite a trilling in her voice, it was not far off. Entering the kitchen, she moved more lightly than usual, appeared almost joyous. Not even the near-empty larder could disturb her. For once she hardly bothered with the ritual of pulling forward to the edge of the shelves the thin lines of tinned food. I always thought the way she regularly readjusted them – to give the appearance of plenty – a little odd for a grown-up. It was the kind of act of magic – like sneaking the last biscuit and puffing out the empty packet – which we all thought we could get away with. But when our mother tried something similar no one was ever fooled. I suspect she really knew that we saw beyond that first line of tins to the emptiness behind but she kept up the pretence. Perhaps she did it for her own benefit. Anyway, there was no need today because soon those lonely tins would have company.

Who would have thought that itching could be so encouraging; but it was. Our mother had a good feeling. She'd never been proved wrong about it. Nonetheless, there must have been some residue of nerves because she rushed to the front door as soon as the postman pushed the post through the letter box. The first signs were not encouraging: the envelopes were brown. 'Pure bills,' she said scornfully. She only half opened them and peered in as if they contained something that was potentially dangerous. We all recognised the routine with this unwelcome mail. After a while someone started calling them 'letter bombs'.

There was still the chance of a second post before lunchtime. Mum announced that she was going to make some cornmeal porridge and, by way of a treat for us, to 'fry two dumpling'. If she did it to distract herself, even that didn't work. Every so often she shouted out from the kitchen: 'Time check?' And when you looked at the clock, it wasn't long after she'd previously asked the time. The morning seemed to be ebbing away, taking some of her confidence with it. You could see the first doubts emerging as she cleared away the breakfast things. The poor woman struggled to hold onto the certainty of our imminent good fortune with the same vigour as when the hand had first begun to itch. The space in her head, vacated by departing money worries, soon began to fill up with an alternative anxiety. Where was this new money coming from? Who would provide it? By 11 o'clock there was still no obvious candidate.

Just a few moments later we heard a sound which though familiar made little sense. Everyone's ears pricked up. Coins were being slotted methodically into the electricity meter – more than a dozen 50-pence pieces one after the other. It had to be Bageye of course, but we were all confused. Even though the money was going in rather than coming out, the sound was as thrilling as an explosion of coins cascading from a lucky pull on a one-armed bandit.

The meter was filling up with enough coins to keep us supplied with electricity for a couple of weeks, maybe longer. Usually, at any one time, just a single 50-pence piece would be surrendered and even then only grudgingly, after the dull click of the meter money running out. There'd be a near-hysterical scramble as the lights went off, until someone answered Mum's call for a volunteer to go and find Bageye and remind him: 'We cyann' live in the dark.'

On the rare previous occasions when our father filled the meter in advance of the electricity running out it meant only one thing: he was bent on taking an emergency bath. Yes, bwoy, not just a quick wash off at the sink but a lengthy soak in a piping hot bath. It was a rare luxury, but there was a catch. To fill the bath you needed a boost from the immersion heater which was known for 'eating electricity'. The rule on bath nights was to be extra careful with its use. Our mother would plead with us to 'take time and kiss the immersion'. But you couldn't expect a mature, long-seed man like Bageye who'd fathered five pickney to make do with warm water. And sure enough, after he slotted his last coin into the meter, Bageye returned to his bed, waited about thirty minutes for the immersion heater to take full effect and then started running a bath.

After a longish soak he emerged at the top of the steps. Freshly scrubbed; moustache trimmed; a generous splash of aftershave on his chin; ready for inspection. Come on, you had to admit the man knew how to turn out. Mum did nothing to disguise her look, which said: *I hope he brock him neck coming down the stairs.* He fired off a round of 'morning's in all directions. No one answered. Though our father was the conductor from whom we took our cue, everyone was apparently suspicious of this uncharacteristic good cheer. 'Wha'appen?' he asked eventually. 'You cyann' say "good morning"?' A chorus of 'morning's rang out like a peel of church bells.

'Hot water still hot,' said Bageye. It was his way of hinting that someone ought to take a bath in his water. Though he gave the impression of not caring either way, it was always best that at least one person took up the offer – best for the majority if somebody made an individual sacrifice. My older brother, Milton, whose turn it was, mounted the stairs with all the grace and enthusiasm of a prisoner taking the final steps to the execution block. The runners on the staircase had been broken long ago, so that the loose carpet was stretched taut and temporarily locked into position as he trudged up the stairs.

Milton always worried that no matter how warm the water after Bageye's exit, there was always a remnant of scum on the surface. But really these islands of greying soapy water were no more disturbing than lilies on a pond. You could also take courage from the thought, as you parted the water and lowered yourself into the bath: *I'm doing this for my father, but also for myself.* Because surely men want to feel good about themselves. I imagined, whenever it was my turn to enter our father's bathwater, that I was being baptised in the Church of Bageye.

Several minutes had passed and Milton was still only halfway up the stairs. 'Listen, old man,' Bageye shouted after him. 'That water gin clear, you hear, so nah bother dirty it up.' I suppose he might have said it for comic effect, but our father was not a man for cracking jokes, so you couldn't be sure. He could have meant that the water was clean enough for another child to follow Milton into the bath. No one would have volunteered. No one ever did. We each harboured the suspicion that any one of us, lulled by the comforts of the still-hot water, might be reluctant to leave the bath when we needed to pee. Hard to prove, of course, as the straw-coloured streaks of evidence soon disappeared, but the possibility remained.

Bageye moved towards the stove. The cornmeal porridge in the pot still retained its liquid state, just about. He turned over the porridge with a wooden spoon, sniffed at it contemptuously, and left the spoon standing in the pot. 'Hear me now.' He wanted us all to know – his wife in particular – that if it was a choice between being served up the 'prison food' of cornmeal porridge yet again or nothing at all, then he preferred to go without. He was a man of his word. A satisfied look passed over his face. Yet you could see almost immediately that he was in trouble. Despite the willingness of his head to make the necessary sacrifice, Bageye's belly had other ideas. He opened the larder, knowing that its contents would not be promising, but he did it nonetheless. He moved onto the cupboards, absent-mindedly at first, but then he was soon pulling them open and slamming them shut like a punter trying to guess under which of the three cups the magical ball was to be found. He returned to the larder and peered into its dark interior. The confirmation of its emptiness was too much. He snapped. 'But wait, not a t'ing else in here to eat?'

Mum pursed her lips, sucked in some air, 'kissed her teeth' as we say. 'Me nah even bother answer you,' she said.

On any other day, war would have ensued, but on this day Bageye was acting out of type. He pulled out his clip. It bulged with £10 notes. He unfolded half a dozen notes, maybe more, and slid the money across the kitchen table. If his face had been a word, it would have been 'there'. Onoo t'ink I couldn't provide for my pickney – there. You doubted me – there. Onoo t'ink you can drag me down in the gutter, think again – there. There is the proof, my friend: six crisp £10 notes. Mum's face went into a kind of spasm of shock. But, curiously, more than that was an expression bubbling up under her skin of a woman wrestling with the onset of tears. Now that the treasure was before her she hesitated. She mumbled something that sounded like: 'I'm not used to this kind of life,' and looked up to the heavens until the tears drained back into the ducts. Mum scraped up the notes without counting them, and shoved the money into the pocket of her apron.

'Bwoy, not even a "thanks",' said Bageye.

There was silence. Not complete silence, of course. In a house with all us pickney, that was not possible, but as close to it as you might imagine. We were heading for 'an atmosphere', as Selma would say. It was certain. There could be no detour. But after minutes of this gunslingers' duel in the sun where no one was prepared to draw first, the solution suddenly occurred to me.

'Thank you,' I said.

'I talking to you?' answered Bageye. He kept his hard gaze on Blossom. 'I talking to she.'

She was not in a talking mood. That seemed obvious to everyone except our father, but then Blossom spoke in a way that showed there could be no confusion.

'I'm not in the mood for you this morning, Satan.'

Those of us prepared to risk raising our eyes from the ground would have seen that Mum had slipped into quartermaster mode. She had no clipboard but moved around the kitchen, opening drawers and cupboards, making a mental inventory of everything that was needed, not just food and clothing but household repairs as well. She couldn't keep it all in her head, or rather, all to herself. Even though talking was off the menu, certain people needed to be informed. She wasted no time in settling on the one subject that was guaranteed to cause maximum irritation: the cupboard with the hinge and door that were barely hanging on.

'That drop-down door want fix,' she said.

'Since when?' Bageye barked. The sharpness in his voice and the sight of the veins beginning to stand up in his neck should have caused Mum to pause but she merely snorted sarcastically: 'Look from when. Since time.'

Bageye's chest wheezed noisily, as if his lungs were demanding another cigarette. He yielded in style. Every gesture was deliberate. Peeling off the cellophane wrapper; opening the packet; removing a cigarette; closing the lid. For a very long time he tapped the cigarette on the packet like a tennis player bouncing the ball as he prepared to serve. It wasn't just the pleasure of smoking; a cigarette allowed him time to think.

You see, at some stage the sight of the drop-down door hanging from its hinges must have grieved him. Opening it wasn't a problem, but closing the thing required a hard-to-master technique that for some reason only Selma had perfected. Bageye, especially, had never acquired the skill. The door mocked him every time. To shut it he settled on force over precision. A few months back, the door had come close to being repaired when Bageye returned with a new hinge sold to him by Joe Burns. But the hinge didn't fit: it was twice as big as it should have been. He suspected Joe had known all along. 'Joe coming like a ginnal,' Bageye had concluded. 'T'ink him can use him brains 'pon me.' A ginnal wasn't just a crook. It was a crook who actually enjoyed his crookedness. Despite the outward assurances, when it came down to it, he just couldn't be trusted. Joe was like the slow-leaking back tyre on his motorbike my father refused to change. Most nights chancing instead to pump up the tyre in the expectation that this time it would stay firm, he would be genuinely surprised – more than disappointed – to discover the next morning that it was flat again. He and Joe had exchanged some bad words over the oversized hinge, and then it was never mentioned again. After a while Bageye must have made a pact with himself to stop thinking about it. It was his way. All in all it was pretty effective. And if any of the fellas, ignorant of the history of the drop-down door, happened to comment on it, Bageye would shrug his shoulders and explain: 'Look how many pickney I have, man. You fix it today, it brock tomorrow.'

But the drop-down door was only the start of Mum's list. What did her husband have in mind, she demanded to know, for the soles on his pickney's shoes that had separated – despite the repeated, generous applications of glue – and continued to slap as they walked to school?

'Already?' Bageye's gaze flicked in my direction and travelled wearily down to my feet, to the toes that were beginning to peek through the tips of my shoes. For a while he said nothing, but not because he didn't want to. He made you think of an actor who'd forgotten his lines. It was painful to watch. Eventually it came back to him, and he spoke, almost as if it was an attempt at a punchline to a joke: 'That boy want iron boots.' No one laughed.

Bageye didn't feel the need to stick around for the rest of the inventory. After all, he knew what was coming. He retired to the living room, and right on cue, we heard him angrily moving bits of furniture around. You could say it was one of his pastimes. After an argument was finished (and sometimes before) he'd start on the rearrangements.

'Carry on.' Mum let out a sad, strangled laugh. She winced at the sound of the gramophone being dragged across the floor. 'Carry on. Look how much you still have leave pay on that little half-dead somet'ing and you gwan mash it up so. Carry on.' All the while she was saying this, Mum was flapping her outstretched hands towards me, in a gesture that I should follow my father into the living room. 'Him might need a little help.' It wasn't entirely clear what she meant by 'help', as, pointing to my shoes, she whispered to me to remember to 'strike while the iron is hot'.

A chair blocked the door into the living room. I could just about squeeze through the gap without disturbing it. Bageye stood on the chair; his arms were stretched above his head towards the ceiling with a pencil in one hand and a ruler in the other. I had always thought my father a big man but, on tiptoes, as he strained to reach the ceiling, it was apparent that, actually, he was quite short. In a year I'd probably be as tall as him. It was an alarming and disloyal thought and, for a moment, I feared my face betrayed the secret, for he looked at me in such a peculiar way. My father was a man of remarkable intensity. He would have made a great silent movie star, for like Mr Knight, he rationed words, especially when it came to his pickney. Bageye expected his meaning and intentions to be worked out from a well-placed glare. Mostly he was right. You always knew when you'd done something to disappoint; only the specifics needed to be filled in like blanks in a crossword puzzle. So it was best to get your apology in early and work out what it was that you needed to be forgiven for later on. It could even be enjoyable – a bit like going to Saturday-morning confession where you received absolution for sins you had made up.

Having squeezed into the living room, I wasn't so sure that I shouldn't try to squeeze right back out again in the hope that my presence would only be registered by Bageye in a 'Did I just see what I thought I saw – no, couldn't have been' kind of way. The reason being that at particular times (and this might have been one of those because you couldn't always judge) the living room was out of bounds, and only for 'big people'. Decorative chaos reigned throughout the rest of the house. In all the other rooms the unprepared surfaces were painted garish colours: lime-green ceilings competed with orange walls. Invariably, air pockets developed on all those walls and the paint bulged until pricked by a child who couldn't resist also picking at the crumbling plaster and sometimes even eating it. The front room, by contrast, was a monument to order. The centrepiece – the drinks cabinet with its few bottles of rum – served first and foremost as a display. A pineapple-shaped, plastic ice bucket sat on the top shelf, designed, Bageye was convinced, for black people. It had to be some kindly Englishman's design. 'After all,' Bageye would concede, 'one or two of them is all right.' No matter the designer, the pineapple ice bucket – too good for ice – was a heart-rending reminder (like coming across a stranger that you're convinced you've met before) of our past life in the Caribbean. The plastic fruit – oranges, lemons and bananas – now widely being seen on market stalls, served the same larger function.

Alongside the drinks cabinet was the most expensive item in the house – the Pioneer gramophone with shelving for a small collection of prized Trojan records. One album in particular – a compilation of reggae songs called *Red Red Wine* – was played incessantly by Bageye at the weekends. The cover featured a cinnamon-coloured model whom we were supposed to celebrate as a Jamaican. But I'd never met any Jamaican woman in England like her, with such long straight hair and heavy, silvery eyeshadow. Stranger and even more disturbing was the pose of this barefoot, waiflike model – sitting on her heels wearing a very short white kaftan, holding a glass of red wine as if she suspected it was poisoned. Of all the records, that album appeared the most special to Bageye, but I don't imagine it had anything to do with Miss Jamaica.

More than the records, more than anything, it was the ornaments that marked out that this room belonged to Bageye. They were treasures from his time at sea and he had a strong, almost childlike, attachment to them. The replica of a ship's wheel with its shiny metallic painting in the middle of the statue of Christ the Redeemer atop the mount at Rio de Janeiro regularly received the attention of Mr Sheen's furniture polish. And no grubby child's paw would be tolerated on the front room's wallpaper whose floral patterns, despite Bageye's numerous frustrated attempts, refused to line up so that the edge with one half of a flower was never satisfactorily matched to the other half on the adjoining sheet.

A door connected the back (dining) room to the front room but it was permanently locked. Not with a key. Our father had devised a far more foolproof method for preserving the front room's sanctity. He'd removed the handles and even the barrel of the lock so that it could not be turned – although it didn't take us long to work out that if the end of a spoon or fork was inserted into the lock and twisted, with a little bit of perseverance, the door would spring open.

My father looked down from the chair, like a priest from his pulpit, and treated me to one of his standard glares.

'Sorry,' I said. 'Sorry for not knocking.'

'Is wha' do you?'

'I just wanted . . .' I faltered.

'Is what you want exactly, mmh?' He couldn't bear the wait for me to respond.

'Yes, Lawd, want it, want it, cyann' get it,' said my father. 'Have it, have it, don't want it.' It was one of his regular sayings. 'If a man want somet'ing and him feel him deserve it, he nah have to apologise.'

'Sorry,' I said.

'She send you? Or you feel for just spend little time with your father?' His irritation was made worse, I felt, by the awkwardness of trying to measure the ceiling; the ruler constantly threatened to slip through his fingers.

It was at times like these that you felt unsure about when to make your move, to act as Mum suggested and strike when the iron was hot, because Bageye gave the impression of having intercepted the order and broken the code; he behaved as if he was in a crowd of pickpockets who, if he let down his guard for the briefest moment, were likely to relieve him of his hard-earned cash.

'You t'ink I'm a millionaire? Where is my Rolls-Royce?'

My father ordered me over to the bay window and bid me draw back the netting and the curtains. He was insistent. He wanted to show me something that would make me marvel.

'Pull it back. Right back.'

Parked immediately outside was his faulty, reconditioned motorbike, next to the neighbour's nearly new Hillman Imp.

'See my wheels there.'

The pity in his eyes was hard to take. The inadequacy of the motorbike had been compounded by the arrival of our new neighbours, the Barkers, and by Mr Barker – the driver of the shiny Hillman – in particular. To make matters worse, Mr Barker was a Jehovah's Witness and on top of everything was the problem of his colour: Buckley Barker was as black as black patent-leather shoes. There must have been more than 500 families on the estate – only two or three of whom were black – yet one day we woke up to discover the council had moved in another black family right next door to us.

'Imagine that,' my father said the day the Barkers moved in. 'I travel over three thousand miles to get away from the bad-minded Naygars, and look who they put next door.'

It might have come across as a kind of embarrassment but it was more the case that my father never liked to make himself conspicuous in front of white people; never liked to draw attention to our colour. I doubt whether Mr Barker was too happy with the arrangement either. They hardly exchanged two words. Despite his complexion, it might have worked out all right if Barker had been a Jamaican, but he was a 'smallee', Bageye informed us, 'from one a dem small island that don't even have name'.

We never did find out which island. Buckley Barker was not going to chat his business with us, nor with anyone really. He was one of those men whose master plan was to get through to the end of his life without being disturbed by too much enjoyment. You got the sense that it had all started to go terribly wrong for Buckley Barker when the fire and brimstone of the Old Testament was replaced by the moral slackness of the New Testament. Closing the door on the Jehovah's Witness recruiters who regularly turned up on our doorstep peddling their faith with an urgent desire to 'save' blacks, the cursed descendants of Cain, Bageye was even more perplexed that the Barkers had signed up for 'that tripe'. He'd shake his head and curse. 'You see how black man stupid.'

And whenever we peered out of the bedroom window on a Sunday morning to see Mr Barker in his stiff tweed suit, solemnly setting off for the Kingdom Hall, Milton and I would turn to each other and whisper: 'You see how black man stupid.' I secretly agreed with my father about Mr Barker, and compared him unfavourably with Summer Wear, who was just as black. Summer Wear's face, I remembered, was as warm as a Caribbean sunset, but from Mr Barker's eyes there was no light at all. He was a sullen little hammered-down man who merely went from home to work and back again, Monday to Friday. Apart from the time he spent improving his car, the rest of his life was measured out in joyless church attendance and DIY at the weekends. He was always fixing something. If Bageye imagined (and he did) that 'the smallee just doing it for spite me', then Mr Barker's endless purchases of car accessories sent my father's resentment into overdrive.

Looking out the window at the newly upholstered seats of the Hillman Imp and the leather sleeve covering the steering wheel, Bageye half turned towards me and cursed his lot: 'When are you people gwan stop put your hand in my pocket?' He pushed the pencil behind his ear, let the ruler slide onto the glass table and reached into his breast pocket for a consoling cigarette. But the cigarette didn't push back the host of unwelcome thoughts that were tormenting him; if anything it brought them forth.

'See my smoke there! When last you see me with Marlboro or Superking? When last? Is pure roll-up me have to smoke. No man, this cyann' work, cyann' go on so.'

He fell silent for a while. Perhaps he'd surprised himself. Or perhaps, more likely, his conscience was pricked by the outburst of sarcasm usually held in reserve for his wife.

'Is all right,' he said eventually.

But his regret, if that's what it was, could not be counted on, of course. It might just as well have been a ruse. If my father's mood was improving, then the sight of my exposed toes would set him back. But the toes were nearly impossible to get inside the shoes. Only after an enormous squirming struggle could I retract them like a tortoise's head into its shell.

My father held out his hand for the ruler and resumed his measuring. 'If the ceiling thirteen foot by fourteen foot and each tile one foot square how much tile we gwan need?'

Bageye feigned ignorance. He obviously already knew the answer, but I was indecently happy to go along with the game. I was torn between immediately revealing my intelligence by giving the right answer and drawing out my response long enough to suggest the toughness of the question and respect for the man who had posed it. It was something of an annoying habit of mine, this demonstrable eagerness to please adults, especially Bageye, which often caused my siblings to cringe. But ultimately it was a chance to match Bageye's charity and restore the good humour that the day had promised.

'Is it, er, one hundred and eighty-two?' I asked.

Bageye nodded with just a hint of satisfaction. The iron, if not burning hot, was warming up again. Mum might not see the merits of ceiling tiles over new shoes or a replacement for the worn-out lino. It would be another example of 'the man pure foolishness' as far as she was concerned. But Bageye would have had his reasons for it; anyway, the man had obviously made up his mind.

'One hundred and eighty-two? We gwan need some reinforcement.' Bageye shouted for Milton to come on out of the bath, quick time. 'Look like him and the bath turn friend,' Bageye said drily. He almost sounded amused but you could tell that if Milton wasn't down soon he was going to catch hell. He should have emerged long ago but he'd lingered a while, as we all did when in the bathroom, hoping to be forgotten about in the sea of interchangeable children until a parent did a headcount or the thought crept up on them: 'Wait. Who missing?' Despite there being no lock on the door, despite the fact that you continually ran the risk of an unexpected intrusion, the bathroom was the one place you'd be guaranteed a degree of privacy.

Our father stood at the bottom of the stairs and followed Milton's descent all the way down. 'What that 'pon your head?' There was a bit of fluff from the towel caught in his hair. 'Is so you gwan leave the house?' Bageye ordered Milton to fetch the brush (whose bristles I always thought more suitable for the floor) to scrape through our half-inch, military haircuts. Without warning, his manner had switched to that of a recruiting officer reviewing some very unpromising material.

'Never can tell who you can meet 'pon road.'

We were subject to a final inspection – our shoes seemed to be exempt – before our father selected his hat of choice for the day. I'd recently worked out that you could tell what was in store for you by which of the dozen hats he chose. The golden brown corduroy cap carried the most hope. The selection of the fedora meant it could go either way. If he picked up the woollen, oval-shaped Russian Cossack hat you were almost certainly done for. Bageye moved down the hallway and plucked the fedora from the coat rail. He appeared to be on the verge of saying something to our mother, but in the end remained silent. Curiously, she, too, held her tongue, and Bageye waved us on through the front door.

Once outside, we trailed behind him, struggling to keep up, as Bageye hurried from the house brimming with optimism like a man who'd been on trial and feared the judge's 'Take him down' and the start of a long jail term, only to hear the words 'You are free to go' instead. From the tortuous route Bageye was taking, neither Milton nor I could work out where we were heading. At one point we followed his lead as he stopped and started to walk backwards, retracing our steps like Red Indians on a breakout with their horses from the reservation, outfoxing the pursuing cavalry.

Bageye, it seemed, was trying to avoid someone, something or somewhere. My guess was that ultimately we'd end up in Bury Park where a lot of the Asian people lived. It made sense as that was where the cheapest shops in Luton were to be found.

We turned a corner and Bageye pulled up so abruptly that we, following hard on his heels, almost banged into the back of him. One of the fellas, Be Still, was sitting on a low wall just down from the Parrot – the local pub that was popular, despite the string of Union Jack bunting decorating the walls, with all of the West Indians in Luton. Bageye didn't look especially pleased to see him but Be Still beamed with his brilliant-white piano-keyboard teeth. He'd had the dentures put in only the week before and had been smiling ever since.

At the time none of us kids could work out why he was called Be Still as he didn't appear to be at all fidgety. It should have been obvious. Be Still hardly ever moved. But it wasn't as if he was a praying Buddha or that he was lazy. Be Still just didn't see the point of unnecessary exertion. If reincarnated, he'd have come back as a Venus flytrap. Once he'd found his spot for the day – say outside the Parrot – that was it: he was happy. You could leave him and go about your business and hours later on your way home, passing by the Parrot, you'd find Be Still unmoved, sitting on that low wall.

As well as his unhurried coolness, Be Still was known as a natty dresser. All of his suits were said to be handmade by an Indian tailor down at Bury Park. He could afford so many suits, it was rumoured, because he got a discount as a man married to a coolie woman. Be Still would 'get vex' if ever he overheard the men passing remarks about his wife; he'd rouse himself from his spot and curse them: 'You talkin' tripe, you hear. If she a coolie then how come she nah have no ring in she nose?' The matter could have been cleared up quite easily once and for all if the fellas had managed to actually see her, but Mrs Be Still hardly ever appeared in public. It was a shame about the wife, Bageye would say, 'but Be Still smart, man'. The Indian woman's people were business people and some of their ways must have rubbed off on him. 'He never like spend money, yet him have two-penny,' said Bageye. If Be Still was cautious, then he was always an enthusiast when it came to spending other people's money.

'Fancy that,' Be Still said as my father approached. 'My mind just run on you, and here you is.'

'And my mind just run on you,' Bageye sighed. Obviously, Be Still was the very man he'd been trying so hard to avoid. Nonetheless, 'give him what he value', as Mum would say, he had his uses. In fact, it was Be Still who'd given Bageye the idea about the ceiling tiles in the first place. He had them in every room of his house. And Bageye asked him now where in Bury Park he had bought them.

'Me? You asking me?' Be Still looked affronted. 'You joke?

'Ceiling tile is not a joke-joke t'ing,' said Bageye breezily.

Be Still held an enormous bunch of keys in one hand, counting them off the ring like worry beads with the other. He didn't look up. 'But what it have to do with me?'

It was strange to see just how genuinely confused Bageye looked. His eyes roamed discreetly over Be Still's Bury Park suit. His mind, no doubt, pictured the Bury Park tiles on Be Still's ceiling back home. You wouldn't have blamed Bageye if he'd decided just to change Be Still's name to Bury Park and be done with it. But he could see the man was riled, and was almost gentle with him.

'Easy nah, me just-a ask,' said Bageye. 'Me hear say—'

'What you hear!' Be Still snapped back. 'Me don't have no passport for go down those parts.'

Bageye shot him a hot, angry look: 'Cho, man, you don' have for go on so in front of the pickney.' He took in a deep breath and let it out again, as you do when examined by the doctor. 'Look from when we been frien'. Me never mean nothing by it. OK? We cool?'

It took a while longer, like a print emerging from the negative, for Be Still's ivory smile to be fully restored. 'Yeah, we cool.' He stopped fiddling with the keys, wrapped them in a handkerchief, and put them in his trouser pocket. From his other pocket he produced a crumpled paper bag of sweets which perfectly explained his dentures. Hammer and chisel might just about have made an impression on them: enamel had no chance. He commanded us: 'Take two. Don' be shy.' Like all of Bageye's spars, with the exception perhaps of Joe Burns and Castus, he treated children as exotic, captive animals, on day release from the local zoo; animals who were miraculously able to talk. Peanuts would have been preferable to the sickly Indian sweets his wife had got him hooked on. Nodding appreciatively, we popped them into one side of our mouths and sneakily spat them out the other, while Be Still stood and beckoned Bageye to follow him just a few yards down the road. Even at that distance it was still possible to decipher from the murmurs just what was being said.

'Me have somet'ing for you,' said Be Still triumphantly.

'No, is all right.'

'Me hear lightning strike last night.'

'Twice,' laughed our father. 'Lightning strike twice.'

'Lucky streak. So you must strike again, me frien',' said Be Still. 'Argument done.' Bageye didn't answer at first. He looked in our direction and after a good long pause – long enough to unsettle even the most confident soul – he said something that both Milton and I found chilling. With his puffy bag eyes locked on us and speaking between draws on a cigarette, he said very, very clearly: 'You mean, strike while the iron is hot?'

'Yes, man, while the iron hot,' answered Be Still. 'Ne must. Wheel and come again.'

The reason for my father's bulging money clip

became clearer as they spoke. Bageye's attempt to lower his voice to a level beyond our comprehension could hardly compete with Be Still's exclamation-mark-studded speech. They resembled parents (one more conscious of eavesdropping children than the other) quarrelling over when to come clean on the existence of Santa Claus. The uneven but lively and apparently theoretical debate focused on whether the luck of a certain man (no names mentioned) at Mrs Knight's poker game the night before could reasonably be expected to hold out till the 3 o'clock at Newmarket.

'Stand Alone have what price?' asked Bageye.

Be Still barked out a set of numbers together with the usual key phrases – 'odds on', 'favourite', 'each way' and 'to win' – that we still found bewildering. It was all the more confusing because Stand Alone or Sea Breeze or any of the runners at Newmarket could so easily have been the nicknames of some new fellas instead of the horses.

Be Still can't have been winning the argument because after much back and forth we heard Bageye conclude: 'Me not too fond of that price, bredren.' He started to move off towards us but Be Still wasn't giving up. He shouted after him: 'Just t'ink about it. Me gwan up the office later. Me can meet you there.'

Bageye seemed to be thinking about it all the way down to Bury Park. We tried to match his erratic stride which slowed eventually to a stop. The thought of what had just come to pass with Be Still was eating away at him: 'You see that man? That man is the Devil.'

Passing the rows of tiny, dirty brick tenement

houses, whose front windows were so close to the street you had to force yourself not to look in, we eventually made it to Bury Park. Outside the hardware shop Bageye hesitated, making some sort of mental adjustment, as if he needed to steel himself to go in. The hardware shop was an imposing structure perched on the edge of Bury Park. One of the most striking things about it was that Englishmen continued to run it. The building and the people had a stubbornness about them. Never mind that the majority of the shops in the area had surrendered to Asian businesses, this proudly English-owned establishment wasn't going to shift. Mostly because the hardware shop virtually had a monopoly in that part of town, it thrived. The workforce of apprenticed youths and slightly older men was constantly on the move, going up and down ladders on coasters which rolled along the walls, fetching tins of paint, rolls of wallpaper and boxes of nails.

The bell above the front door sounded a welcoming peal when we entered but the more senior men on the counter hardly looked up. They seemed almost indifferent to the need to make sales. All had the off-white skin colour of a life spent mostly indoors. They were serious, almost grave, and looked, I thought, like doctors. Except they wore grey coats instead of white, and had tape measures draped around their necks where stethoscopes would have been.

Bageye walked briskly over towards them. His eyes settled on a set of hinges in a box on top of the glass-covered counter.

'How much that value?'

The salesman looked over the rim of his spectacles.

'The price is on the label, sir.' As was often the case with English shopkeepers, the 'sir' didn't sound as if he was being polite, though you'd have been hard pushed to make the accusation stick: Englishmen were overly polite to the point of rudeness. Bageye never got the hang of it.

'That's not what I asking,' he said a little more forcefully. 'I asking how much it value.'

The shopkeeper freed one of the price tags. 'A guinea, sir,' he answered precisely. 'The price is a guinea.'

'It don't value a guinea,' argued Bageye.

'Well, that's the price, sir.'

'For one?'

'For the pair.'

Bageye sighed. We squirmed, even though he'd explained on more than one occasion the difference between the price of something and its worth. He didn't believe in price tags. They were merely suggestions of a thing's value, which could only be worked out in negotiation, preferably with the man who'd actually made it. Our father kissed his teeth and asked: 'How much for one?'

The shopkeeper, having first chosen not to understand Bageye, was beginning to enjoy himself. His lips barely contained the ironic smile that dribbled out of the side of his mouth. 'They come in pairs, sir.'

'I don't need the pair. Just want the one.'

'One minute, sir. I'll just consult my colleague . . . Harry?'

Harry, who plainly considered himself something of a front-of-house diplomat, came over. 'Something the matter?'

'We don't sell single hinges, do we, Harry?'

'No, George. We most certainly do not. We sell pairs, George. In this country we sell pairs.'

'Would you like a pair, sir?' asked salesman George.

Bageye told both George and Harry that the hinges would keep for another time. It didn't make sense to buy a pair when he only required one. He'd wait until the other hinge went on the door and needed replacing. Ceiling tiles, however, were another matter. He wasn't going to leave the hardware shop without them.

'You have ceiling tile?'

'In bundles of twelve, sir.'

'How much we need?' my father asked me.

'One hundred and eighty-two.'

'Just the one room is it, sir? Only that's an awful lot of tiles. How many is that, Harry?'

'Over a thousand, George.'

It was difficult to work out whether this was part of the impromptu comedy routine both seemed bent on indulging in. Bageye's reddening throat was like a tightening knot. He endured all of the slurs, including the suggestion that he'd probably want patterned rather than plain tiles because, as the salesman enthused: 'They're proving popular with our West Indian clientele.' Bageye peeled off a couple of notes and slapped them down on the counter. The transaction was complete but he didn't budge. The salesman made a 'What, what is it?' gesture with his hands palms up.

'The receipt,' Bageye growled. There was raw pain and anger in his voice. 'What about the receipt?'

We left in a hurry with the snatched receipt, a tub of adhesive and a dozen bundles of plain tiles. Each of us had a bundle awkwardly trapped under each arm;

the other six bundles we held by the knots of the strings which bound them like presents. A bus ride would have been sensible but, equally, would have been dangerous to suggest. Bageye was too quiet. He reminded me of those unexploded fireworks you are advised not to return to – just in case.

The polystyrene tiles slipped and slid over each other, squeaking as we marched away from the shop. Caught by sudden gusts of wind, they threatened to fly off, escaping the string used to tie them in bundles. Far greater balancing skills than we possessed were required to keep them intact. And because of the mood in which Bageye had left the store, the consequences of dropping the tiles were too awful to contemplate. We struggled on, probably longer than was wise, before slyly readjusting the string. We needn't have worried because Bageye was too preoccupied to notice. He only realised after quite a while that we were lagging yards and yards behind, and shouted over his shoulder, commanding us to pick up the pace: 'Quick time. Quick time, now.' Though we were definitely in retreat from the hardware shop and Bury Park, Bageye's internal compass seemed to be steering us further into town and not towards the safety of home. He slowed on the approach to Coral's, the bookies. If you thought that Coral's was an unlikely scheduled stop on the way to Farley Hill, then you didn't know my father. That much was expected, but Be Still's presence was not.

By a miracle neither Milton nor I could fathom, Be Still emerged from the bookies just as we came to a halt outside. Not enough time had lapsed, for a man of Be Still's tortoise speed, for him to have arrived before us. But there he was, smiling at Bageye as broadly as his lips would permit, like a priest welcoming a returning, penitent sinner. *Star Trek* offered the only rational explanation: the humanoid, Be Still, had been atomised outside the Parrot pub, teleported to the steps of Coral's and reassembled.

Our father ordered us to put down our loads. He arranged them in two columns so that they were as high as post boxes, and just about level with my eyes. We were each assigned one of these towering, tottering edifices. 'You can manage?' Bageye asked. From his look, 'no' was not an option. Be Still reached into his pocket for the bag of sweets but Bageye briskly and noisily rejected them on our behalf. A fella like Be Still should have understood that there came a time when a gift started to look more like charity. Bageye's children were his own, not orphan pickney in need of another man's sweets. Our father held out some coins which Milton, springing into life, was given charge of dividing in two. It was a tantalising prospect. This rare, spontaneous generosity called for immediate action, but then we were also instructed not to move from the spot. 'Don't let anyone trouble you,' Bageye cautioned. 'Me soon come.' He turned and disappeared with Be Still through the plastic strips of curtain which adorned the door to the bookies.

The Queen herself could not have expected more from the dutiful sentries stationed outside Buckingham Palace. Neither of us spoke. Not because we were on pretend guard duty. No, neither of us wanted the jinx that would surely result from expressing the anxiety we both felt: that Bageye's 'soon come' meant we were in for a long haul and, therefore, there was every likelihood of the unthinkable: that we'd miss *The Waltons*, which was due to start in under an hour.

We were all enthralled by *The Waltons*, spellbound by the simple but idyllic lives of the family who had no luxuries but, equally, never suffered real privation. If yams, rice and potatoes were staple foods at Farley Hill, then *The Waltons* was staple TV. It vied for most popular programme with *Little House on the Prairie*. Us kids had never missed an episode of either programme.

A further frustration was that the real-life drama unfolding within the walls of Coral's was not open to us. Even more than Bernard's junk shop or the shop with the partially boarded-up front that everyone knew sold second-hand dirty magazines, Coral's was alluring and mysterious. It was partly because there was no way to see into the bookies: the windows, painted white on the inside, were opaque. But of greater curiosity was the actual working of the bookies. Like church, going inside changed you – if only temporarily. The men entered the building in a state of conspiratorial excitement, and exited, mostly, head down, reading their futures in the pavement.

Mine and Milton's eyes were fastened on the curtain, monitoring the slightest tremor of the strips that might signal our father's return. Every time a punter pulled the curtain to one side and ducked out of the betting shop, a burst of animated race commentary leaked through the strips as if someone had suddenly turned up the volume. For a brief moment you could see inside – men on stools, staring presumably at a screen – before the strips of curtain swished back into place. The men looked shifty and perplexed when they saw us, as if they'd been caught doing something they'd thought, until then, they could have got away with without confessing.

After about an hour, the novelty of sentry duty was beginning to wear off. In the absence of anything better (or anything at all) to do, Milton started cranking up for one of his ridiculous propositions. He made what he thought was a strong case for a bet. We were both to turn around, turn back, look at the strips of curtain for a second and then turn away from them.

'Right,' he said. 'Let's bet on how many there are of one of the colours of the strips. Let's say blue. Blue OK with you?'

I nodded, though I suspected that Milton, as usual, was several chess moves ahead of me.

'How much do you want to bet?' he asked innocently, holding up the coins for which Bageye had made him banker. 'Half OK with you?'

'OK.'

'Actually, you owe me tuppence from the time before, remember? Double or quits? Might as well. We'll toss a coin for who goes first.' The coin, of course, fell in his favour. 'Right, you first. So how many blue strips, do you think?'

I didn't have to think. I told him that there were four strips. He plumped for six. I wandered over to the curtain to count them off. Four precisely. 'Just as I thought.'

'No, no,' Milton scoffed. 'You must be colour-blind, old man.' He held up a couple of green strips beside the blue. 'You see this? You do see this, don't you? Oh, dear, hard lines, sonny boy, hard lines. Four and two make six, if my memory serves me right.'

'But those are green,' I pleaded.

'Not strictly correct, hombre. More of a bluey green, don't you think?'

'Yeah, blue-green.'

'Not green, then?' Milton argued. 'But blue-green. Blue-green. You said it. Game, set and match.'

Milton made a fist with the coins inside and shook them triumphantly. I lunged at him, grabbed his fist and tried to wrestle it open. Both towers of ceiling tiles immediately tumbled over, and, with exquisite timing, Bageye and Be Still emerged through the curtain of plastic strips.

The Art of Sticking Up
Ceiling Tiles

B AGEYE STEPPED OVER THE FALLEN pile of tiles as
a man might straddle a drunk lying in the gutter
– with only half a thought to offer assistance. Finally,
it would have been undignified, so that was that. He
put out a hand to stop Be Still, who apparently had
no such qualms, from bending over. Milton and I
quickly repaired the piles but our father was not
happy with the realignment. He was a fever bursting
to be expressed. The betting shop remained oblivious
to the calamity outside, thankfully. And the stranger
who passed by did so without looking in our
direction. Yet Bageye clearly nursed a feeling of shame
that would not be denied even though there were
no other witnesses. He spoke almost in a stage
whisper: 'You cyann' stand up straight?' Some coded
words passed between Bageye and Be Still that
seemed to calm him. I guessed they were finalising
plans for a possible reunion later in the day. Once
the columns had been straightened to our father's
satisfaction, he picked up his share of the load and
marched the few yards to the number 4 bus stop.
Within a quarter of an hour we'd arrived back at
Farley Hill.

We got off at the stop just twenty yards down from
the house. Ordinarily, Bageye would have insisted on

alighting at the earlier stop. Even though it was at the top of the road and much further away from our home at number 42, getting off there meant our father wouldn't have to walk past the yard of Mr Walcott at the end of our block.

The Walcotts completed the trio of coloured families on the street. But my father did not entertain Mr Walcott: he reserved a particular dislike for the man even though he was a fellow Jamaican, christening him 'Boasty Morgan'. In the first instance, there was Mr Walcott's smugness over his corner house to contend with. Black people as a whole might have been cursed but Boasty Morgan was one of those fellas who was born lucky. Just like that, the council had presented him with a corner house. And annoyingly, not only was it semi-detached but it also came with a much larger garden than all the others. Boasty carried on as if it was a cut above the rest – which it was – and almost as if he owned it, and was not a mere tenant like his less fortunate neighbours. The expression that he nearly always wore on his face was a measure of his good fortune: it reminded you of a cat whose smile revealed the canary trapped behind shiny fangs. Mr Walcott seemed friendly enough to me and my brothers and sisters but Bageye said he was only 'skinning him teet''.

Whenever he saw you coming up the road Mr Walcott would find some sudden reason to rush out of his house to his neatly tended garden and begin fussing with some flower whose beauty couldn't be improved on; or adding a dash of paint to a fence that was already brilliant white. For houseproud orderliness and practical handiwork Mr Walcott made even Mr Barker look like an amateur. But whereas Mr Barker barely spoke, Boasty Morgan's boasts were carried on generous lips that were a perfect fit for his deeds and many, many achievements. Why he wasn't called 'Boasty Walcott' we never knew; and nor did we take the trouble to find out. Everything about him was boastful. When he spoke he had the habit of raising one side of his top lip like a snarling rock'n'roll singer to reveal a front tooth ringed by shiny slivers of gold.

Mr Walcott's tolerant understanding and acceptance of his own expensive tastes for luxurious inessentials did not extend to any suggestion of waste on the part of the rest of his family. The man was insanely tight. Once when I asked his son about a nasty cut and bruise below his right eye, he looked back into the house, then said: 'I spent my dinner money.'

Our parents were not surprised when they heard about it. But it wasn't Boasty Morgan's reputation as a child-beater that incensed and united them: it was his 'jump-up attitude'. I say 'united', though they never shared their views with each other. Boasty Morgan was 'too damn conceited, you hear', Mum would tell her church sisters whenever he stopped her and drew her to one side to give an account of his latest triumph. Answering questions about him from his spars, Bageye would tell them: 'Yes, is facety, him facety.' He was much too facety (facetious), especially when Bageye considered, as many did, that back home Boasty Morgan's people were 'country people who dig hole for pit toilet'.

Mr Walcott, who both the church sisters and Bageye's spars grudgingly reminded themselves was a 'good colour', was mostly damned for his pursuit of white people; he even boasted about the number of them he had as 'frien''. Yes, it was common knowledge that he was 'white-minded'; and though he'd never been caught saying it directly, it had leaked out that he wasn't too keen on his children playing with us. 'Imagine that,' Bageye would snort whenever the subject came up. 'The man pickney too good for my brood. What kinda foolishness dat?' Bageye would conclude (and Blossom would be in total agreement) that when it came to Boasty Morgan and his blind ambition for his children: 'Every monkey t'ink him pickney white.'

When we'd alighted from the bus the coast was absolutely clear: there was no sign of Mr Walcott. But as we edged closer to his house he suddenly popped up like a meerkat behind the whitewashed fence. Our polystyrene tiles caught his attention. He leaned on a pole, wide-eyed and amused.

'Bwoy, you good, that is not a easy something. If it was me now, I wouldn't business with tile. In the end you're penny wise and pound foolish. Why you don't just Artex the lot and done with it?'

Bageye wondered aloud why Mr Walcott didn't just wind in his neck and let us go about our business. He was sorry to speak to the man 'hard' in front of his boys but enough was enough, man.

Mr Walcott was taken aback. He wanted to know why our father was being so 'ignorant'. He really wanted to know, and continued his enquiry all the while we walked silently past him up to our own house.

★

'We reach,' announced Bageye as he put the key in the front door. It was a relief, of course, having run the one-man gauntlet of Boasty Morgan, but it was unusual for Bageye to suggest as much. Sometimes when he made such simple statements it sounded like an opening, as though there was a chance for you to join in. But you couldn't be sure. Once or twice I'd muster the courage to act on it, building on something my father had said, but it usually met with a poor outcome – a gruff silence or worse, a curt question about whether something was wrong with me. And if Milton was watching it all unfold, at the end he'd wander over to me and whisper 'pitiful', a word that he'd recently learnt and tried out a dozen times a day. Even so, I suspect there was something more to the unnecessary announcements from Bageye. If you listened carefully you could definitely hear something else in and around them. The trouble was that, on those rare occasions, the way he spoke was so subtle that it was never picked up on. It only occurred to you later. His voice then had the slightly hoarse quality of someone trying to drain it of emotion. I couldn't have told you when I first noticed it. But once you registered it in Bageye's speech, you heard it all the time. Needless to say there was no response, no shout of recognition on our return, as we squeezed through the front door with our polystyrene bundles.

'We reach,' Bageye repeated a little less coolly, actually with a touch more heat. He looked perplexed rather than vexed. Sometimes it didn't seem fair. It was as though he was the only one in the audience who didn't get the comedian's joke. You see, Bageye was unaware that the sound his pickney's ears were always most keenly listening out for was not him coming back into the house but rather the click from the lock of the front door closing which meant, mercifully, that he had left.

'Is where them is?'

Neither I nor Milton spoke. No one seemed to be about. If you gazed, though, as I did, down the corridor towards the kitchen, you could just make out – behind the curtain (similar to the bookies') hanging over the doorway – an eye peeking through the strips. The eye belonged to Mum. She was still and watchful as Bageye pushed open the living-room door with his foot, and we, his two silent porters on this last stage of the gruelling expedition, were commanded to follow him inside. I tried to signal to the roaming eye in the curtain about the outcome of our trip. I shook my head, only slightly so that it was undetected by Bageye but pronounced enough for Mum to take note. By doing so, I hoped she'd understand that the mission – to buy shoes or anything else practical – had not been successful. She blinked but kept on looking to make absolutely sure that there could be no mistake: it seemed impossible, yet, if she'd searched her heart, it was not unexpected. Her husband had left home, his pockets bursting with money – and had returned not with shoes, coats or satchels for his pickney but with ceiling tiles. Mum did not speak but sort of mumbled under her breath like the faithful at church, 'Oh, hallelujah.' It was not an expression of praise; more one of exasperation.

Yet my own traitor's heart swelled with an excitement – one that I didn't want to own up to

– at the prospect of new tiles on the ceiling. What a vision. It was a start; the beginnings of a more perfect future at Farley Hill. And my father, doing that trick of reading my thoughts, agreed. 'Not everyt'ing can fix one time,' he said.

Without pause, Bageye began to create a space under the hanging lampshade in the centre of the room. I was allowed to use my father's penknife to snip the cord holding the bundles of tiles. Bageye took a biro and carefully drew a thin line, an arc, around the edge of a tile. His steady hands were even more noticeable when – following the line – he carved out a tiny polystyrene wedge with the knife. He stood on a chair and held up the tile to the rim of the centrepiece covering the light fittings on the ceiling. He repeated the process until he had four tiles which when joined together formed a perfect hole in the middle.

Our father wasn't exactly an action man but he wasn't one for dallying. Perhaps Be Still had given him some advice. He handled the tiles confidently. Using a scraper, he applied the wet cement-like adhesive to the back of a tile and then kind of slid it into position, pressing it firmly onto the ceiling with his thumbs and knuckles. If there had been a plan, you'd have said that things were going smoothly.

My brother and I were so caught up in Bageye's unexpected mastery that we'd almost forgotten about our favourite television show. But gradually we became aware of the coincidence of the time with the unmistakable sound pulsing from the dining room of the first bars of *The Waltons* theme tune – as simple and plain as the dungarees worn by John-Boy and his siblings. Somehow, impossibly, it brought on a deep nostalgia in all of us children. Each time the theme tune came on it seemed capable of making us swoon. During the Great Depression of the 1930s, in the shadow of Walton's Mountain, John–Boy, Jim–Bob and their extended working-class family gave dignity to dirt. Poverty was not a crime: it was a noble test to be endured, just as we endured. Walton's Mountain was very far from Farley Hill, and yet, at the same time, it was not. The attractions of that show were never commented on and with time would begin to wane, but for a brief moment in 1972 it held us all in its powerful grip and caused us, for instance, to commit ourselves to the satisfying round of wishing each other goodnight just as the Waltons did at the end of each episode.

''Night, Selma. 'Night, Milton. 'Night, Shirleen.'

The start of *The Waltons* tested our commitment to the ceiling tiles. The sound leaked through the walls and under the door between living and dining rooms. It was maddening to imagine the others settling comfortably into the settee as the credits rolled. But how to get out of the task in hand? Both Milton and I saw the dilemma reflected in each other's eyes. It was going to be every man for himself. I'd have to think fast.

We had no way of knowing how long the job of sticking up the ceiling tiles would take. To speed up the process Milton volunteered to apply the adhesive to the back of the tiles. It looked simple enough but actually it was rather like spreading peanut butter on cream crackers. If you were not careful the crackers cracked. Milton was not as cautious as he might have been. The very first tile broke in two, as did the next one. After the third explosion Bageye had had enough. 'Is what do dem?' Bageye seemed to address the ceiling. 'What is wrong with my pickney?' He looked soulfully at the damaged tiles. 'Onoo, not satisfy till you bankrupt me. Put it down, man. Right now. Give him the somet'ing.' He ordered Milton to hand over the scraper to me. 'You only a-waste my time. G'way!' Milton was banished from the room but before he was in the clear Bageye shouted: 'Is so you carry on? Onoo just pick up and gone when you wan'?' Milton stopped abruptly. 'May I leave the room?' he asked, perhaps a little too keenly. Bageye waved dismissively at him, cursing as he left: 'Is not one time monkey want wife!'

'Yes, man, is not one time monkey want wife,' Bageye repeated now, more for my benefit, I supposed. You didn't need to know exactly what his words meant to understand what was being said. 'You see, onoo?' He stamped on the chair. 'You hear dat?' He thought about stamping again. The chair wobbled and he steadied himself.

'One day the other foot gwan drop.'

All I could hear was the word 'onoo'. It was a very bad sign. 'Onoo' was a Bageye word which filled you with dread. He only used it to describe us when he was especially vexed. I never liked to hear it as it carried some unnamed threat. Something was coming, as sure as an itch would be scratched. I didn't, though, begrudge Milton his exit. If it was a deliberate strategy then it was risky and he deserved marks for it. It might have been just a series of accidents but even so. Once you were out, you were out and didn't look back. Everyone knew the score. Of course, further escape would be nearly impossible. Bageye was now primed. I resolved, in my head, to be the best spreader of glue on ceiling tiles that there had ever been.

It was a funny business, because after a while you realised that once you accepted that there was no alternative but to surrender to your fate, it wasn't so bad. Not exactly what you might call fun, of course. 'Fun' would have been stretching the point. After all, I wasn't that different from my siblings. At some level we all felt uncomfortable about the prospect of spending time in Bageye's company. You looked forward to it as you might after-class detention with Mr Jablonski, a troubled sadist with impeccable teaching qualifications. But, as I strained to hear the sounds of *The Waltons* bleeding through the walls, a curious thought worked its way deep into the marrow of my bones: next door, John-Boy was helping his pa down at the sawmill, and here we were, Bageye and son, working similarly in silent communion (nothing needed to be said) making improvements to Farley Hill. How about that?

And Bageye was turning out to be something of a natural in the art of sticking up the tiles. Each square of polystyrene successfully attached to the ceiling was a minor triumph. He let out a pleasing sigh before beginning again. The pattern, though, was difficult to define. My father was partial to random bursts of inspiration. One tile followed on from another as the mood took him, so that the effect reminded you of the haphazard design of letters slotted together to form words on a Scrabble board.

74

'What you t'ink?' he asked, but I knew it was a trick question. Bageye would not welcome any suggestion departing from the course he'd already set out on. I nodded encouragingly. He was not convinced. Only when he stepped down from the chair for an inspection, to check on progress, did he seem suddenly aware that it might have been more practical to build up one complete line of tiles at a time. The mistake was to have started in the middle. As we approached the edge it was obvious that the tiles were not square with the wall but at an odd angle, creating a dizzying optical illusion that made your eyes cross. Bageye looked equally mystified.

'I wonder if it the wrong tile the man sell me?' My father called for the tape measure and bid me write down the numbers as he called out the length and width of one of the tiles. 'Twelve inch by . . . wait, what the rass, twelve inch.' He shrugged. 'Well, so it go. If it no go so, it almost go so, right, little man?' He stepped back and rolled his eyes sheepishly towards the ceiling. 'Actually, it nah too bad, you know.'

Another man would have cursed his luck; would perhaps have pulled down the existing tiles from the ceiling and started again from the edge of the wall, but not Bageye. We ploughed on.

My father had completed about a third of the ceiling when his pace began to slacken, until finally he came to a halt. He looked as if his mind was adrift. Something troubled him: his face was fixed in that familiar expression when the memory of some other task he was supposed to be carrying out wrestled with the anxiety of being unable to recall exactly what it

75

was. It must have come back to him because he eventually scraped off the glue from the next tile and hurried out of the living room and into the dining room where his unexpected entrance caused a flutter of dismay and panic among his pickney scrambling to get out of the line of fire. All were confused. Bageye rarely set foot in there except occasionally for breakfast or Sunday lunch.

I waited a little while before following him. By the time I arrived, Bageye was bent over the television, roughly handling the dial which switched the channels. He clicked and *The Waltons* disappeared. An educational programme with scientists in a chemistry lab filled the screen, and then another click and we were onto the fuzzy 'ghosting' channel that was always impossible to tune. The second time round our father clicked on each setting with even greater determination, spinning the dial almost through 360 degrees till it was in danger of snapping. John-Boy and Co. made a fleeting reappearance, and were gone again. There was a collective groan from the settee crowd – muted but still riskily audible. Bageye slapped his palm onto the top of the TV set and miraculously a picture emerged (albeit briefly) before being swallowed up by the storm of grey dots once more. In that flickering second, our father's viewing choice was glimpsed: the afternoon's televised horse racing from Newmarket. Jockeys and horses had vanished but the muddied sound of the commentary remained. Milton was quickest to see the opportunity, volunteering to climb into the attic to adjust the aerial. Now that was quite pitiful, actually. Bageye never answered him. Our father was happy to make do with the measured but quickening disembodied broadcaster's voice over the rumble of hoofs on turf as the horses turned into the final furlong.

The commentary slowed to normal speed once the runners crossed the finishing line. The names meant nothing to us. Our interest was solely on what the placings would mean to Bageye. But at such times, he never gave anything away. You had to know what to look for, and not be too impatient. Sure enough, a short while after the winner was announced, Bageye kind of nodded and quickly pulled his head back like a man who'd caught himself falling asleep.

The sun and the clouds had been playing hide-and-seek all morning. Earlier the sun had been peeking through the cobweb of clouds high in the sky but now beyond the net curtains you could see it had started drizzling again. The commentary crackled back to life, announcing the start of the next race, and I slipped away and headed towards the living room.

I was surprised to find Mum in the living room with a basket of coiled, damp and steaming sheets and blankets recently washed and wrung out in the bath. Even more surprising were her features. She gave the distinct impression of having been caught doing something she'd rather not admit to. We both knew she'd been admiring the tiles. Mum swept out of the room just as Bageye breezed back in. But he did not resume the task of putting up the tiles. Rather he began clearing things away, scraping the adhesive onto the rim and back into the tub. He was painfully aware of doing wrong but looked not as if he was about to head off to confession and ask for absolution: defiantly, he was hell bent on sin. Everything should

77

be left just as it was, he'd soon come and finish off the tiles, he said. Thrusting eager arms into his jacket and pulling on his favourite corduroy cap, Bageye hurried out of the room. The front door slammed shut after him, and I watched as one tile and then another groaned, lost its grip and floated down from the ceiling to the floor.

It Drive Well, Eh?

BAGEYE WOKE WITH A PLAN. You could tell
because he had 'the look' which generally
frightened the arse off us kids. Sometimes it just came
on him like a fever. Like, damn it, man, he'd had
enough and was 'done play'; like when he'd get fed
up with the total mess of the house and embark on
a blitz to make it regimentally spick'n'span (at least
for one day), and we'd all be given previously
unheard-of chores such as polishing doorknobs that
would not see a duster again until another outburst,
maybe a year later.

Yes, man, Bageye awoke early without the need for
any child to rouse him. He only ever did so when
he had a burning bush of a plan – one of those
'nothing will ever be the same after this day' life-
changing moments that he'd probably been nursing
like a last drink at closing time for quite a while now.
It was a plan that would require some intelligence in
its execution, which went some way to explain the
determination that was in his eyes and all about him
this morning.

The fug of family life that had clouded his vision
was banished and gave way to a clear blue sky. This
morning, timid he was not. No, sir, despite what others
thought. And believe it or not, he knew their thoughts
sometimes even before they did. Because everywhere

he saw limits or those who were trying to impose limits on him. He heard whisperings that he would 'never amount to anything'. No names mentioned but one of the authors of that anti-Bageye campaign had lain down in the same bed, that's right – get this – had lain down in the very same bed with the man for years. For more than a decade she had gone to sleep not thinking well of her man, thinking he was nothing, would never be anything.

Bageye glanced at us like a man who was suddenly aware that he'd been overheard talking to himself. But so what if we'd heard? It was about time that we knew that he knew. You didn't have to tell him, Bageye knew. He wasn't born yesterday. Yes, you heard it before but you better believe it this time, 'cause it forty-eight years ago he born. He was aware that he was the butt of the joke which went something like: 'Bageye? But if he was gwan do somet'ing with him life him woulda done it from time.' No, no more. All of us must leave all that negativity at the door, check our holsters at the entrance to the saloon bar, because this day change was a-coming. Because there comes a time in a man's life when he can put off the plan no longer. How did I know? How did common-sense little man know? Well, it didn't take long for the details to emerge.

'When last you see your cousin?' Bageye asked. By cousin, he meant the children of *his* cousin, Darcus. Everyone knew the answer but no one dared remind our father of the overheated argument and curses that had fouled the air the last time the two men met. Darcus had accepted a red-hot racing tip from Bageye and over the phone had asked our father – no, make

that *pleaded* with our father – to put on a bet for
him. Bageye would be able to take what Darcus owed
him (plus a little somet'ing for the tip) out of the
winnings. But the horse didn't even place and Darcus
had gone back on the agreement. Darcus claimed it
was a bad tip; that Bageye, as usual, had persuaded
him against his better judgement, so he'd flatly refused
to pay. Imagine that! When the fellas heard about it,
it wasn't long before someone had christened Darcus
with his new name: 'Scandal'.

It could not have been that Bageye had forgotten
his cousin's dishonourable actions, and yet now a visit
to Darcus's was being planned. None of us had a clue
as to what was going on, not even Selma who usually
prided herself on being at least a step ahead of all us
kids. She gave off that air of being too preoccupied
to venture an opinion to her tiresome brothers. She
was, no doubt, on one of those missions from Mum
that neither Milton nor I, having failed once too
often, could be trusted with. I suspect she had tagged
along simply to act as a reminder to Bageye, to be
his conscience. But on this day our father paid little
attention to any of us.

Along the way to Darcus's house, he seemed
occasionally to revert to talking to himself, to be
making some mental preparation, like a boxer tapping
his forehead before the bout. His strange mood
presented me, Milton and Selma with a dilemma:
strain to hear what Bageye was saying just in case an
answer was demanded, or stare blankly ahead (Milton
and Selma's preferred option) to forestall the possibility.
All the while our father played back the argument
over the racing tip, reasoning it out, as he had done

now for almost a week. But still it could not be explained. A few hundred yards from our destination, he seemed finally to have worked it out. He turned and announced: 'You nah know how water go pumpkin belly.' That was it: some things made no sense. Of course, how did the liquid accumulate in a pumpkin? Nobody knew. He shrugged as if resigned to the double loss – his own and Darcus's wager: 'If it go so, then so it go.' After days of being at the mercy of a raging fever, the fever had broken.

Darcus owned a house up by the airport. I say 'owned' but we were careful not to use that word in front of our father, though it didn't stop Mum. She just thought it worth pointing out that Darcus had arrived in England several months, almost a year, after Bageye and yet he already had a mortgage and house while Bageye was still paying the council rent.

'Him nah own it outright as such,' Bageye would explain. 'Mortgage company own the t'ing for true. Actually speaking, it more of a borrows, until the one time him miss a payment and them send bailiff after him, and then is puke him puke. Own? Which part? Check this, me frien', "own" mean say him have it on the never-never. Time him finish pay for it, worms will have gone with him.' At such times, Mum would listen (her face flushed with disbelief) but eventually she would surrender the argument. In answer to her husband's faultless logic she could find no words.

Darcus's house was tall and narrow. The living quarters began on the first floor, above the garage, so that when you knocked it always took a long time for someone to traipse down the steep staircase to the front door. I suppose it was modern but Bageye thought the architect must have made some kind of mistake.

'Wha'appen, Darcus?' Bageye asked as Darcus wearily pulled the door ajar. 'Is how you do?'

'Not as good as you!' Darcus snapped back. It was what he always said. After all, why was it anybody's business how he was doing? What did they want? What were they really saying? Darcus was expert at turning the most innocent greeting into a malicious taunt. The 'how do you do?' might just as well have been a curse. Nobody else could see it, but to Darcus Sullivan it was obvious. Darcus was the most suspicious man you were ever likely to meet, and the list of suspects was endless. He suspected the timekeeper at Vauxhall's of docking him hours that he had sweated and worked, and denying him the chance for overtime. He suspected Mr Maghar of secretly taking out one or two matches from a box of matches and selling the box to him as if it contained the full set. Darcus never left Maghar's shop without counting the matches. He suspected his wife, Merlene, of saving the bigger pork chop or fillet of steak for herself. He suspected us children with runny noses of contagious diseases that he needed protection from. He suspected everyone, but the person he most suspected was his cousin, Bageye. In his dealings with Bageye he carried on as if they were in the middle of a long-running board game where he, Darcus, was equipped with simple draughts while Bageye bamboozled him with moves from knights, bishops and other chess pieces.

Blood, Bageye often reminded us, was thicker than

water. But Darcus never seemed to share this view. At Mrs Knight's poker game, outside the pub or betting shop, whenever any story arose about our father, Darcus would spring up from nowhere and join the argument: 'Bageye? That man tell too much lie, you hear.'

Darcus spouted his theories about his cousin even when we, Bageye's pickney, were present. And as my father would say, I didn't especially dig that. Uncle Darcus would have been unaware of my feelings, of course, because as a rule us pickney didn't talk with big people, and Darcus never spoke to children, even his own brood, not directly: all conversation went through his wife.

Darcus was saved by Merlene. Joe Burns spoke for many of the fellas when he said: 'If it wasn't for the wife, me wouldn't business with him.' You could say Merlene was almost one of the fellas. Her popularity came from the fact that she was both a glamour gal and a tomboy, mixed together. She had one of those full-throated laughs that some people called dirty. But you forgave her. You forgave her everything. She didn't belong in that odd, sterile house with that little rat-toothed man for a husband.

We climbed up the steep stairs into the open–plan living room, and were confronted by the type of carpet where you immediately start worrying about your shoes. Quite a few of the fellas were there already, swigging back rum or bottles of stout and talking over each other. Merlene came towards us, sashaying along an invisible catwalk, accompanied in my mind's eye by the silent, dying tremble of cymbals. She folded us into a hug, first Milton and then me, but Selma backed away when she tried to embrace her. Instead she held out her hand, and laughing, Merlene took it and curtseyed.

When Merlene straightened she reeled me in once more, and fixing Selma with a twisted-mouth expression of mock hurt, she said loudly, more for the audience than for me: 'Come again. You can have the one meant for she.' And amid the guffaws from the fellas, she added: 'Which one is you again?'

'The third one,' I answered as drily as possible. Even so, there was, I noticed, that croakiness in my voice that appeared when I was hurt or disappointed. No matter how hard I'd been training myself to mask it, the voice usually gave me away.

'Yes, this one my favourite, man.' She tried to make it into some kind of joke but the funny thing was I knew that, at that moment, despite her earlier betrayal, I *was* the most important person in the room to her, and always would be. Though nothing more was said, it was our secret. Only years later would the truth emerge that I wasn't alone in harbouring such thoughts: Merlene had that same effect on all of the children – except for Selma, of course. Selma liked to carry on like a big person – unimpressed by most things and most people. According to Selma, Merlene was able to return from the airport with armfuls of booty – miniature bottles of alcohol, soaps, biscuits – not because she was, as we all understood, an air hostess, but rather a cleaner, cleaning out the planes after they landed. She may not have impressed Selma, but among the fellas there was an undignified jockeying for position whenever Merlene, with her almond-shaped 'Chiney' eyes and treacle-coloured skin, made an entrance. She had power over them. Plenty of men would have swapped with Darcus, even though he complained that he had married 'one of them gal that not satisfy till she suck the marrow out of the bone'. Merlene cast such a spell on the men that you suspected, one day, she would have to pay for it: Darcus would have no choice but to beat her.

Merlene bid us make ourselves comfortable whilst she went off to fetch some bun-and-cheese. Darcus's eyes tracked us all the way to the red settee. It was a three-seater, new, and made from leather, though you couldn't entirely be sure of the leather part as it was still covered, a month after its arrival, in the transparent plastic sheath that it had been delivered in from the manufacturer. We all understood that the settee – leather or not – was not for sitting on. You'd no more sit on the man's settee than you would use his new toothbrush. So we lowered ourselves onto the plastic covering the way a mime artist would have: it was pretend sitting. Actually, if we could have managed it, Darcus would have preferred us to have held our positions, like Olympic gymnasts, just above the seats for the duration of the visit. But the strain was too much. There came a point when you had to give in, and admit to yourself that actually you wanted to let go. It was like giving in to the urge to be the first to pierce the silver-foil top of the milk bottle even though you didn't want a drink; or the compulsion to topple the tower of playing cards you'd spent ages erecting. Not only was it too much to keep everything just so, but it was better, more fun to watch it all come tumbling down. And anyway, as I allowed gravity to take hold and pull me ever more dangerously towards the cushions, a comforting thought popped into my head: *So what if we sat down on Uncle Darcus's precious settee. What could happen, what could possibly happen?*

I'd kept Bageye and the fellas under close observation, watching their lips twitch and curl, and counting the burps and belches bursting on their rum and whisky breath; it was amusing at first, until they reached double figures. Three or four men was all it took to turn Darcus's living room into a bull pen. Here there were half a dozen. Mostly, I'd not really been able to make out, from their raucous overlapping voices, what was being said. Occasionally, though, a few words broke free from the crowd, as Bageye's did now. Though his tone – that of someone struggling to remain even-tempered ('To hell with it, man') – was disturbing, more freakish was what our father was actually saying, and the fact that he'd probably been saying it all along: 'What could happen?' Bageye was demanding to know from his cousin exactly what he was afraid of. 'What could happen, what could possibly happen?'

'That's what I 'fraid of. When you say there not a t'ing to fear, that's when I tek fright.' Darcus must have been pleased with how the sentence had turned out because he laughed, albeit tentatively at first but then more loudly with the encouragement of the others. If perhaps the hilarity seemed forced and unbelievable then that was because Darcus rarely said anything to produce such a reaction.

The fellas were still drying their eyes when Merlene returned with a tray of snacks. 'Don't listen to him, you hear,' she teased. 'Darcus take fright morning, noon and night. You want see fear? Watch him face when he sit 'pon toilet and find not enough paper there.' That set the fellas off again on a round of rolling, goofy guffaws.

Merlene soaked up all of the bonhomie and laughter temporarily loaned to her husband. You could almost feel sorry for Darcus: it was all over so quickly; his face returned from paper to stone; from an uncharacteristic cheerfulness to its more usual thunder, but he didn't risk saying anything to his wife in front of the fellas. That would come later. Merlene continued to make her air hostess's way smoothly round the room, giving out the snacks to us pickney (winking slyly as she did so) and freshening the drinks of the fellas.

Despite the lightness that Merlene brought to the room, the tension between Bageye and Darcus remained. Every so often the cousins caught each other's eye, though neither, it seemed, was willing to venture into a conversation when unsure of the direction it might take. Eventually, Bageye took a deep diver's breath.

'So, old man, wha'gwan?' he asked.

'You tell me,' answered Darcus.

Bageye looked vexed, and for good reason. In my father's books, you didn't invite a man into your house and treat him so rank, even if there was some beef between you, and especially if you were blood. Most times now, Bageye would have 'roughed' him back; would have told him at the very least to 'go to France' (which I presumed was the equivalent of hell). But he seemed unusually at a loss and said nothing so that we were all relieved when Joe Burns suddenly attempted a joke. Joe had been poring over the racing pages in the newspaper with his pen poised, tapping out a beat on his pearly white teeth. He looked up briefly now and stifling a smile behind the paper asked: 'Scandal, man, who you fancy in the two thirty at Aintree?' It was the first time that Darcus had heard his new name, though the fellas had been using it for almost a week. He pushed Joe as to its meaning and when Joe gave it to him straight, Uncle Darcus was ready to run Joe out of his house, and had to be restrained by Bageye and Merlene.

All the while Joe had remained studying the form of the horses. He barely peered over the top of the paper as Darcus lurched towards him. Man, Joe was cool. Ice-water ran through his veins. Let's be honest, you couldn't really intimidate a man who had locomotive pistons for arms. And everyone knew – Darcus more than most – that he wouldn't have tried too hard to break free from those restraining hands: he was only bluffing. It all seemed a little false, like the play-acting of wrestlers on TV, lunging at each other across the ropes – one inside the ring, the other outside. And it also made you think Darcus could have been just a little more grateful towards his cousin, but he shrugged off Bageye as he tried to put a reassuring hand on his shoulder.

After the commotion was over there was a final bit of funny business with Joe that involved him attempting to give Merlene a slap on her buttocks as she passed by with the tray. He obviously meant to miss but caught her with a heavy thwack. And for a brief moment it made me wonder about the phrase I'd often heard the fellas use when they referred to

Joe, that he was 'a cock that never leave any one of the hen untouched'.

Darcus relieved his wife of the last two miniature bottles of whisky and emptied them into a thick, shallow glass. 'Bwoy, you lucky,' Darcus shouted over to Joe, recovering some of his good nature. 'Next time I just give you two lick in your neck back.'

It was one of the things I most liked about the fellas: they'd made it a point of honour that no one was ever allowed to bear a grudge – not for too long at any rate. The mood had mellowed so much that Bageye began working the room, clinking glasses with each of the men, Darcus last of all.

'No,' Darcus barked out, anticipating a question from Bageye. 'If it's the wheels again, the answer is no.'

Darcus was right about the wheels. Bageye needed wheels because obviously a man must have transport. Bageye had the need and Darcus the means – a car that he himself couldn't drive.

Ever since he'd come to this country, Uncle Darcus had had trouble relating his bewildering new life in England to the old certainties of Jamaica. He'd chosen Bageye, or was it – he couldn't now recall – Bageye who had offered his services as guide through the mysterious workings of council-house waiting lists, licensing laws and the social. Grateful at first, in time Darcus had come to feel that our father was not entirely open in his dealings with him. For instance, Darcus's share of the little brown bag of special tobacco which Bageye got for them each week never lasted Darcus more than a few days. It was understood, I once overheard Darcus explain, that Bageye thinned it out by way of compensation. 'After all, is him tek all the risk so me wouldn't begrudge him a pinch,' Darcus had said. 'But him nah know say how far pinch measure.' What apparently upset Darcus was that nothing had ever been agreed from the outset. When Darcus stopped to think of it, he realised that Bageye was hardly ever explicit about anything. No arrangement was ever watertight. 'He and I cousin,' Darcus would feel justified in repeating, when quizzed about their relationship, 'but the man tell too much lie.'

You tried to push away such thoughts but they crept in, found their way in, like water through a crack in the ground. And you thought, well, yes, from the hesitant way Bageye sometimes started a story, you got the sense – although you didn't want to admit it – that what he had to say might only be true in part. Then you worried about how he managed to juggle all those truths and half-truths, and file most of them away in his head. It must have been an effort to remember not to tell X to Summer Wear because he had told Y to Anxious, and if Anxious was to run into Summer Wear they might get talking and then there was the real risk that Anxious might inform Summer Wear that Y was in fact X. Or was it the other way round?

One night I had a dream that Bageye asked me to file away all of those half-lies; and when at a party he snapped his fingers and called for the first story, I gave him the wrong one by mistake so that he ended up actually telling the right things to the wrong people. From this he'd concluded not that he should no longer tell lies, but that there was little point worrying about who knew what and when. If you thought about it, it made a lot of sense.

When he thought really hard about anything, Bageye's mouth usually gave him away; it twisted like a wrung-out wash rag. He ought to have known from the way that Darcus stared at him now that he needed to relax his face. Did Mum's taunt play on his mind? Did he consider the injustice of their increasingly contrasting fortunes? While he was want it want it, cyann' get it, his cousin, who just a few years back was cutting up car tyres to use as shoes, never seemed to want for anything. Banish those thoughts, my frien'. Bageye was not going to give in. A man, though, could get to thinking, scaring himself in the process, that maybe, just maybe he couldn't get it because he didn't really want it. Maybe he was attracted to the idea – the scent of a woman without the woman, just the hit from one last cup of coffee without drinking it or the cigarette without the aftertaste – and not the actual thing.

He looked out of the window with doleful eyes, down onto the latest unattainable object of desire parked on the forecourt – Darcus's hired Cortina.

'Grass soon start grow from the wheel, old man.'

'If it gwan grow let it grow,' Darcus fired back. 'I fed up now.'

Uncle Darcus's annoyance stemmed from the maddening fact that he didn't know how to drive and had persuaded Summer Wear to rent the car for him. But Summer Wear, inconveniently, was still languishing on an acute ward up at the L&D Hospital. Bageye turned slowly from the window.

'Is not everyone who have licence can teach, you know.'

'Ahhah. Aye, sir.'

'Some of them bwoy pass the test,' Bageye explained. 'But them just like a half-educated fool.'

'I'm telling you!'

'Take me, for instance.' Bageye tapped himself forcefully on the chest. 'Me don't have no education to speak of but everyone know me is a natural teacher. Take this car business. Now, if you really want to learn fast, fast, well, bwoy, I wouldn't look too far.'

'How you mean?'

'How you t'ink I mean? Me could teach you, you know.'

'You have licence?'

'No man, me don't have no licence.'

'Then how you gwan teach?'

'Me have exemption – with the bike. Once you have one licence it can double up.'

'Is first I hear.'

'Bwoy, you think the man gwan tell you? How you think the Englishman get where him is, get all that empire and t'ing? By let you in on the secret? No man, he must keep you where you is, ignorant, a-feed off the scrap from him table. You t'ink him gwan tell you anything but shit?'

'I move slow,' said Darcus, cutting his eye after him, 'but I think fast.'

Bageye crouched down to adjust a troublesome shoelace. He was suddenly irritated. The lace snapped.

'That is your biggest problem. You think too fast. And turn things over too much. Englishman have you just where him want you. And when it time for action you cyann' even fart.' He straightened, giving up on the shoe.

93

'Well, I done fart with you.'

Bageye raised an arm and rolled his shoulders as if he were putting on the jacket that he'd somehow forgotten he was already wearing. When that ensuing battle was won, he pressed each button slowly into its designated hole. He turned up the collar in an overly deliberate fashion and, looking over his shoulder, muttered: 'Right then, me gone.' Bageye started inching out of the room, but before he reached the staircase, Darcus was at his side, pulling on his sleeve, coaxing him back into the room.

'Ease up, spar.' Darcus gently stripped the jacket from Bageye's shoulders and pretty soon was begging him to be his driving instructor.

If you stopped to think about it that was how things often worked out between them. The situation would look dire at first. But give him his value, Bageye had a genius for extraction. Give him time and he'd work the problem out. Naturally, this was cause for celebration. Bageye eased a hand into the jacket pocket and took out what looked like a tiny brown envelope.

'You have paper?' he asked.

Darcus nodded towards the kitchen. Bageye followed him and all the men, and Merlene, filed behind. It was another half-hour before we could leave in the yellow Cortina hire car.

I survived the torment of Selma's and Milton's eyes burning into the back of my head. It didn't seem to matter that I hadn't asked to sit in the front passenger seat but had been volunteered by Bageye to ride shotgun. There would be a period of reckoning with the two of them when we got back home but probably no more than low-grade taunts about my obvious scheming to worm my way into our father's affections. But the limits of assuming pole position among the pickney were quickly exposed when pulled up outside 42 Castlecroft Road and were all bundled out onto the pavement before Bageye sped away as if at the wheel of a bank robber's getaway car.

Four or five hours later there was a knock at the door from a figure whose silhouette was the one my mother, all the time that I'd known her, had seemed most to live in fear of. The shadowy apparition behind the frosted glass was much more terrifying than the Grim Reaper who, as surely as day followed night, was destined to call. Mum pulled open the door and there it was: a uniformed policeman greeted her. She was so alarmed that at first she didn't understand what he was saying.

'Mrs Dixon? I have some news about your husband Ian.'

'Ian? You mean Ian Dixon, Summer Wear?'

'Yes, Mr Dixon.'

'Summer Wear, you mean?'

'Yes. I'm afraid your husband's been involved in an accident. The car's been written off but he's not too badly injured. He's been taken to the Luton and Dunstable Hospital.'

'Why you insist on calling me Mrs Dixon? Me not name Dixon.'

'Oh, I just assumed you and your husband were married.'

'We are married.'

The policeman must have thought she was in shock.

He reassured her that Mr Dixon would be discharged soon. He'd had a lucky escape. Trying to overtake a bus, he was met by another coming in the other direction and the Cortina had been sandwiched between the two.

'That man tek too much chance.' Mum sighed.

The policeman agreed. Firemen had cut Mr Dixon out of the car but he'd emerged with only a few bruises. And everyone on the scene had agreed there was only one word for it: a miracle. There'd be an inquiry later, of course, but that was just routine. The main thing was that Ian, the hospitalised Summer Wear, had not been hurt. Just then Blossom twigged what had happened: that Bageye (who had no driving licence) had assumed the identity of Summer Wear under whose name the car had been hired. And then my mother was really afraid. Soon the hospital would realise that there was already an Ian Dixon on another ward. This was the day she'd been dreading all her life. Her husband, she was convinced, was going to prison. And didn't her own mother warn her not to marry 'the evil wretch'? And look what misfortune he had brought to the house. Not only was he going to jail, but wait a minute, she was implicated now, and she'd be going to jail also. She started to wail.

'Anybody see my cross! Anybody see my cross!'

Mum's cross was too heavy to bear. The policeman was moved by her distress. He tried reassuring her that the inquiry would be a mere formality. As the car was hired, it would have been insured. Back and forth went the discussion with Mum now worrying over the length of the prison sentence and the officer struggling to convince her that no one was going to jail. After a while a strange thing happened: I noticed that Mum was now answering to the name Mrs Dixon without contradicting him. Finally the officer brought the conversation to an end, promising, then pledging on his life and the memory of his dead mother, that everything was going to be all right.

Bageye didn't come back that night. Just as we were going to bed, Mum popped out to the phone box and called the hospital but he wasn't there either; he'd been 'released as a "walking wounded"', the nurse had said.

   Bageye still hadn't returned twenty-four hours after the accident. This, in itself, was not unusual. But there was something odd going on. During the course of the day one or two folk had swung by the house reporting to have seen or to have heard about a man who bore an uncanny resemblance to Bageye, behind a wheel, driving around town. Mum thought it was nonsense and that the 'carry go/bring come' gossip-mongers should clean their glasses for a better look and wash out their ears. But then Mrs Knight came to the house to collect the dues on the pardner money and said something similar. Mrs Knight never made things up or repeated tall stories: she was petite, wiry and serious, and as reliable as a high-street bank manager. In a way, in collecting the 'hands' from all the partners in the pardner money system who otherwise couldn't get loans from high-street branches, Mrs Knight was our unofficial banker. If Mrs Knight said something was so, then it generally was.

In the dream you do not wake to the sound of knocking at the door. You are, after all, dreaming and asleep and the rat-a-tat-tat is part of the dream. But then the knocking persists and you begin to emerge from the half-dream into full consciousness and you realise that someone actually is at the front door. Well, so it was with the car horn. The dull and distant blaring was so unfamiliar and unexpected in Castlecroft Road, especially outside number 42, that at first we did not register it. Until it became apparent that that horn was outside our very door, and summoning us to it. Still, only hesitantly did we peel away from the television.

A sparkling green metallic Mini estate was parked in front of the house, its engine running. Uncle Darcus sat in the driver's seat. It was he who was responsible for the car horn which went off every time Bageye was about to say something to him. The Mini was buffed – given the second-hand-car showroom treatment – and polished to a point beyond that which seemed possible. Even so Bageye ran a chamois leather lovingly over it, the way a trainer might groom a prized horse by running a brush over its belly. It was as obvious as it was unbelievable that the car belonged to Bageye. He winced as Darcus, failing to depress the clutch fully, crunched through the gears. Bageye looked over to the crowd of his children admiring the car from the doorstep. He said nothing but jumped back in beside Darcus. 'You there stroke the t'ing. You have to push down on the clutch.'

Darcus tried again. This time the crunch was even more grating.

'The other foot! The other foot!' Bageye screamed. 'You Jamaicans nah know left from right.'

Bageye turned off the engine. He argued that Darcus would have to familiarise himself with all aspects of the car before switching the engine back on. Darcus had something more immediate in mind. He'd have been quite content to slap it straight into the highest gear, rev it as much as possible and take off from zero to 60 mph in the bat of an eye.

'Familarise my arse,' Darcus cussed. At least that's what it sounded like, but on reflection it was more likely to have been 'familiarise to rass'. I always admired the way the fellas used bad words. It never really sounded as though they were swearing; just that they were vexed and wanted you to know. He turned the key once more.

'Don't mek me get ignorant with you,' warned Bageye, switching it off again.

Darcus jumped out of the car as if he'd been stung by a bee, shot his cousin the most furious look, and marched off down the road towards Longcroft Hill. He was met, coincidentally, by a procession of fellas in their vehicles on their way to Castlecroft Road. They greeted him with their car horns but he didn't stop. Outside the house, two cars pulled up, one neatly behind the other; and then a third turned up and even more fellas piled out. They'd all heard about Bageye's purchase and were bent on joining in the excitement.

'Ahh, it this?' asked Joe Burns, emphasising the word 'it', and making no attempt to disguise his disappointment.

'Look how many pickney the man have.' Joe addressed the group. 'And he end up with what – a Mini?'

'Not even a Zephyr?' Castus asked, going along with Joe's teasing.

'No.'

'Or Zodiac?'

Joe borrowed Castus's glasses for closer inspection. 'No, man, it look a Mini for true.'

'But him nah need Mini. Is Maxi him want.'

'Ahh, true.'

Bageye didn't laugh. Our father had reached that stage in his life when he didn't feel obliged to laugh at something if he didn't find it funny. A car, as far as he was concerned, was not a joke-joke t'ing.

For as long as anyone could remember, Bageye had been the same age: he was forever forty-eight. That was what we guessed. It was impossible to know for sure because our father never celebrated his birthday – well, not in our presence anyway. I had built up the idea in my head that when I grew up I'd buy him the one present that would give him most joy: a car. Bageye had the house, the wife and children. None of them made him particularly happy, but he still held out the hope that a car might change everything. Bageye brooded over the ownership of a car the way some women are said to brood over having a baby. It gnawed at him, especially as there were so many undeserving who already had cars.

He'd put up with the motorcycle but it didn't really suit him. Around the fellas he exuded a kind of looseness, bluffing that nothing could beat the bike for the freedom it gave you. Nothing beat the bike, not even the car. He and the fellas were always running jokes about it, but walking back to the house he would tighten up. If you were out somewhere with him, it became very noticeable. With every step nearer the house the 'good fellas' self would start to recede, and you'd think: *What the hell happened?* At least when Dr Jekyll turned into Mr Hyde there was a reason for it. It could be accounted for. The potion did it. But there was no such explanation for Bageye.

Now my father had a car, I had to let go of the dream of that future gift, but at least it might mean that now, at long last, he'd be less cantankerous in the mornings; disinclined to stomp around the house in one of his dark moods; happier to come home after work or a visit to Mrs Knight's; more prepared to sit down and attempt a normal family life with his wife and pickney; an end to Mr Hyde. He revved up the car.

'How it drive?' Castus wanted to know.

'It drive well,' answered Bageye with just the right hint of modesty and confidence. It was bound to drive well, because my father had a feel for cars. A lot of people said so. I suspected the car was a bonus from his winnings at Mrs Knight's poker game from the night before, though he never let on. It would have explained why he hadn't returned from the hospital.

Finally, someone asked the question they'd all been waiting for, and had skirted round till now: what did Joe Burns think? All eyes were on Joe. If anyone knew about cars it was Joe. After all, the man was a long-distance lorry driver. He gestured to Bageye for permission to inspect the vehicle, and Bageye gave his nodding approval. Joe took his time but there was always grace in his actions. He popped the bonnet and all the old boys gathered around. Joe pulled at some rubber tubes near the top of the engine. Castus gave a running commentary.

'Him checking the spark plugs.'

Joe drew out a long, thin metal stick. He called for a rag; wiped it as if cleaning blood off a sword; thrust it back into the engine and drew it out again.

'Oil check,' whispered Castus.

Joe released the prop and let the bonnet slam shut. Before we knew it he was on the ground under the car. He sprang up soon after. Still not saying anything despite the expectant look on everyone's faces, Joe popped his head through the driver's-side door and looked at the speedometer. Finally, he straightened up and cleared his throat.

'That mileage a little on the high side, you know, Bageye.'

It was all he said but it was enough to spark some mutterings from the group. My father flicked away any concern.

'It have a new engine.'

'New or reconditioned?' asked Joe.

'T'ink it a new recondition.'

'Wha'? Must be Englishman sell you? Let me guess. Is Englishman sell you, right?'

Bageye declined to answer. He didn't have to. He knew as well as anyone that an Englishman was never going to give you something for nothing. Even so Bageye was loath to accept it as the absolute truth. It sparked some excited intervention from the fellas.

'Not a t'ing change from time,' said Pioneer. 'From I come here you nah catch me inside any Englishman business. Jancra pick the bone. Englishman same way. You cyann' blame the Englishman. It just him way. You remember Captain Morgan? And who the other one? Hawkins. Him name Hawkins. Aye, sir. Back in the day, the Englishman give the bredren a few beads and tek away the man island! You t'ink anything change? Not a t'ing change, my frien'. Better off dealing with Paddy.'

'You plan on driving far? How far you plan?' Joe chuckled.

He didn't chuckle for long though. You see, there came a time with my father when you didn't joke with him, and though I didn't see how it happened the warning light must have gone off in Joe's head because all of a sudden he shut up, and instead started giving tips about which junctions Bageye should avoid because Babylon liked to lie in wait in their police cars for motorists there.

Joe's advice carried added weight, especially as Bageye had no licence on account of the trivial detail that he'd never learnt to drive. Learning would have meant handing over money to an instructor; paying for insurance, road tax, MOT, every little thing. So Bageye never bothered. On top of which, Bageye knew how to ride a motorbike. Sure, he may not have passed his driving test but – as I heard him once remark to Joe Burns – given that he knew how to ride a motorbike, 'How much more difficult could it be?' It amounted in his mind to the same thing but it led to certain idiosyncrasies in his handling of the vehicle. For example, unsuspecting passengers were sometimes unnerved to witness Bageye at the wheel, leaning into a turn as the car rounded a corner.

'Excitement finish,' said Bageye, attempting to bring the discussion to a conclusion. He'd had enough of the audience. The early evening light was making way for dusk. The men also grasped it was time to

103

go when ten or fifteen minutes had lapsed and Bageye still hadn't invited them in for a drink. Their leavetaking, heavy on the car horns, was as noisy as their arrival. After the last of them had disappeared, we were told to run and fetch some cushions. Bageye was going to take the family out for the car's maiden voyage.

There were only two seats – for the driver and front passenger. The back seat had been removed. This would have been necessary in any case as five children had to fit into the back. Bageye opened its van-like back doors and we children started to fold ourselves in, heeding our father's warning against squabbling. The biggest child would have to go first, as Bageye would have to get the balance, like the ballast of a ship, just right. We were all about as excited as anyone could remember being in Bageye's company, though there was a reflexive twinge of disappointment when we climbed inside. The interior was neat and trim up front with fake mahogany strips on the door panels, but gave way to a bare shell without even carpet at the back.

Despite the promise of splendid comfort up front, Mum took the passenger seat reluctantly. She wasn't just sceptical about the outing but petrified. Vestiges of worry over yesterday's encounter with the policeman still clouded her face. Then there was the anxiety of her husband driving with no MOT, no insurance, no road tax, no driving test, no nothing. Bageye's own peculiar driving technique topped off a final layer of terror.

Rounding the first corner, us pickney were thrown around in the back like so many sacks of potatoes.

The bone-rattling continued all the way to the edge of town. It might just as well have been the edge of the world; in fact, it was − none of us had ever ventured further. Bageye hadn't thought about bringing a map. Throughout the drive, he scrutinised the road signs, but no matter how much he squinted they became no clearer. He could read them all right, but he just couldn't make sense of them. An arrow to the right led him to drive straight on. The straight-ahead arrow often took the car down side roads or into cul-de-sacs. One wrong turn later and Bageye found himself bewilderingly confronted by three lanes going in the same direction: we were on the motorway.

We crawled along, his hands tightening on the steering wheel. Other motorists shot past and thundering lorries rocked us with a sickening turbulence. Some of us started to whimper. Mum was all for turning back. Bageye never answered her but emitted a low and continuous growl, and when that failed to shut her up, the monologue began. He'd been waiting, he said, for her to start her noise. Why was it up to him to drive *and* read the signs; all her heavy breathing was fogging up the windscreen, and why oh why did she have so many pickney anyway?

Mum began to pray, and miraculously within a couple of minutes her prayers were answered. Without understanding how, we found ourselves on a country lane. Our relief, though, was short-lived. There were no street lights, and the countryside wasn't green, pastoral and idyllic: it was black and ominous. More so when, inexplicably, the car started to slow down, even when Bageye put his foot to the floor. The car was losing life. The headlights dimmed and the lights on the dashboard faded and then disappeared.

Bageye hefted himself out of the car, popped the bonnet just as Joe Burns had done earlier, and for about ten seconds gave a passable impression of a mechanic who knew what he was doing. Mum was ordered to turn the key in the ignition on his instruction. There was no sign of life, even after a second and third time. After a few minutes it was apparent that he was holding out for a miracle – for a mysterious transformation that could be brought about simply by lifting the bonnet.

'The man say, "It drive well. Just need a little tuning,"' said Bageye in answer to Mum's silence, while another thought slowly crept along his brow.

'Wait. Backside! I wonder if it sugar?' He turned a cap somewhere on the engine. 'Rahted! It look say sugar in there.' He was speaking directly to Mum but her thoughts were elsewhere: she remained silent. He was mocked by her silence.

'You can stay there and laugh.' Bageye said it accusingly as if he suspected her of some guilt. I had never seen my father panic. It must have been panic but it came out as rage.

'The car drive well, man, but sugar in the engine. Someone sabotage the engine.'

Lino

IT TURNED OUT TO BE the first and last family drive. Although the maiden voyage had been a setback to husband-and-wife relations, the overall effect of the car on Bageye's mood was positive. This was partly because overnight he started moonlighting as an unofficial taxi driver for some of the fellas who still hadn't made the leap to car ownership. Bageye so loved being behind the wheel that he would have driven them for free but it must have proved a money-spinner because after a while, more people (some strangers to him) started to ask for rides, and Bageye even began making suggestions about home improvements.

Soon he was regretting ever opening his mouth as Blossom increasingly dropped hints about private school for the children and pressed him on the need – painful as it was – to buy a piece of lino for the back room. It got so that he went to bed with the word 'lino' ringing in his ears, and woke up with lino, lino, lino still on the agenda. Until the day came when we were definitely going to look for a piece for the back room. At least that was the plan.

Bageye woke irritably in the morning to yet another strong reminder from our mother that he'd been promising that this was the day. 'You start already?' said Bageye. 'Not even have breakfast and you start already.' He rifled angrily through a kitchen drawer, picked up a knife and began to peel an orange, as his wife laid before him the unarguable fact that he couldn't put off buying the lino any longer, especially as the pickney were going to get sick from sitting on the cold floor from morning till night. She finished her piece and waited for him to speak. Bageye continued to concentrate on the orange until all the skin was removed and the unbroken kiss curl of peel dropped into the bin. She tried again.

'You never hear? Is you same one promise.' Bageye didn't blink. He took it all in as a newsflash that, until now, had been kept from him. He cut the top off the orange as some people cut off the top of a boiled egg. Only when he'd munched his way through the entire orange did I see, through the crack in the door, that he was heading towards us.

Everyone assumed innocent positions on the floor or settee as his head came round the door. His eyes fell on the cracked and degraded lino. He scanned the room for culprits, and half muttered to himself and half declaimed: 'Not even six months and dem mash up the t'ing so?' We children were careful not to catch his eye, but at the same time trembled at the consequences of being caught looking away. He shouted in our general direction: 'Carry on! You pickney gonna bury me and you will bawl when them screw down the coffin lid.' It was already 9 o'clock, yet the heavy curtains, Bageye noticed, were not fully drawn, contrary to the rules. It could only mean that something was being hidden. He tugged at the curtains and exposed the crack and pebble-sized hole in the window, above the sill, that had still not been fixed but plugged with newspaper taped to the glass. A week had passed since that particular catastrophe. Bageye had forgotten about it, and he pulled back now from opening up this new avenue of discontent. He cast his sad bag-eyes over his offspring and singled out me to keep him company on the journey that he was suddenly determined to make. At least it would get him out of the house. He turned to those who'd be left behind: 'And nah bother long down your mout.'

Bageye mistook the sour faces of my brothers and sisters for disappointment when really their expressions were designed to put him off choosing them. I hadn't yet perfected the look. My father favoured me, because, as he often declared to the others, even though I was only ten: 'That boy is a common-sense man.' I was told to run a comb over my head and put some shine on my shoes, quick time. Bageye, meanwhile, adjusted his paisley scarf – he wore it like an English gentleman – and put on his brown corduroy cap, telling anyone who cared to listen: 'When you don't see me I'm gone.' You had to admit the man had style.

Of course, we never addressed our father as Bageye. That was a pet name given him by the fellas. The legend was obscure to us. Only years later did I make the connection with a harmless condition doctors call 'subcutaneous oedema'. Now, looking back, it shouldn't have been the mystery that it was to us, although no one questioned its origins. He'd had the look from the age of sixteen or thereabouts, apparently. Once the bags first appeared under his eyes as a young galley boy at sea, it wasn't long before some wag had christened him 'Bageye'. And the name stuck. He could no more change it than he could the colour of his eyes. It was never soft-sounding, and on the wrong teasing lips it carried an added sting. You could tell that Bageye wasn't in love with the name but if he resented it he never said. It wasn't exactly a term of abuse yet it wasn't an affectionate name either. But then everyone had to have a name. Bageye's was probably on a par with 'Pumpkin Head' and 'Anxious'. No one was as popular with the men as Summer Wear but I reckoned that Bageye, despite his name, was a close second. He was like a balloon inflating whenever the fellas came around the house, but the air would soon begin to escape once they'd departed.

Outside, Bageye ran the chamois leather over the roof of the car before he got in, slipping behind the wheel. He turned to inspect how I intended to close the passenger-side door. OK, it was only a second-hand Mini estate. You, personally, might not think much of it, but Bageye didn't work all that overtime at Vauxhall's and all those night shifts just so that us pickney could slam off the door. His scrutiny, though, did pose a slight dilemma because if you pulled the door too gently then it wouldn't close properly. And, bwoy, as far as my father was concerned if you hadn't managed on the second go then it was best to pretend that you had.

Slide in, close the door firmly, look straight ahead and whatever you do don't ask where we're going. Those were the essential points to concentrate on. 'Let we check by Bernard first,' said Bageye. It was what he always said when anything, any appliance or piece of furniture, needed to be replaced. Bernard was always the first stop even though he vexed my

110

father's spirit. Bernard's bargain store was crammed to the rafters with second-hand treasures. It required some purpose and determination to squeeze through the heavily fortified front door into the cornucopia of goods salvaged from house clearances and pawned items that were never likely to be redeemed. Bernard had not mastered the art of stocktaking; there was always an imbalance between stock bought by him and that which remained to be sold. A man with a more subtle mind might have felt mocked by the electric fires, rugs, pots, pans and array of assorted, unwanted goods that had taken up permanent residence in Bernard's bargain store. Not Bernard. He puffed out his chest with all the proprietorial pride of the owner of an upmarket boutique. But Bageye knew – and you'd be a fool to try and tell him any different – that 'is pure junk inside. Is t'ief, Bernard t'ief, and one day them gonna burn down him kiss-me-arse shop.'

There was no way, of course, that we could go straight to Bernard's. Bageye would have to check by a few of his friends first, call in on his spars along the way. We settled into a nice rhythm with Bageye doing all the talking. I was very well versed in the rules of my father's world, and equally conscious that the rules could change at any time. Just a few minutes into the journey, Bageye wanted to know how his son felt about a piece of carpet instead of the lino. 'Man to man, I'm asking you.'

'Carpet would be nice but . . .' I felt my way to what should have been the right answer: '. . . isn't it too expensive and surely, lino or carpet, us kids will mash it up the same way.' It was a good response.

'You see your mother? Credit! That woman just love credit. Never know a woman love credit so.' He eased back on the accelerator, the better to take the subject in his stride. 'A man must pay his bills before he can allow himself the smallest luxury.'

It was no surprise then that we seemed to be heading in the direction of Joe Burns's. While most of my father's friends, like him, were lean and tidily but modestly built, Joe Burns had arms that bulged like Popeye's after a can of spinach. He had taken a Charles Atlas course and turned out magnificently. But more than his athleticism, it was his generosity that impressed our mother and us kids; only Bageye demurred.

Bageye was still smarting from heroic Joe's latest unwelcome intervention into our lives, dropping off a free bag of corn on the cob at the house a few nights back, when Bageye was on the night shift. The way Bageye saw it, he didn't ever remember asking Joe to bring that stinking sack of corn on the cob to the house in the first place. Though Joe said it was a gift, Bageye shuddered at the shame of his wife letting Joe leave empty-handed. 'Imagine that! How you feel that make me look?' moaned my father. 'A long-seed man like me cyann' provide food on the table for his pickney?' At this point Bageye demanded to know exactly what my mother had had to say on the matter. He wasn't asking his son to 'carry go, bring come', to betray any secrets. He just wanted to be sure that she wasn't turning all five pickney against him.

It was clear Bageye was only going to ask the once, and I calculated that my mother wouldn't blame me for what I was about to admit. That as far as she was concerned, she didn't understand why, when Bageye had so many pickney hungry, with their shoe-backs breaking down, why he, Bageye, would no doubt end up giving money to Joe Burns, and, worse still, more than Joe had paid for the offending corn on the cob in the first instance. Bageye pushed down hard on the brakes and stopped the car. 'Listen, bwoy, when it comes down to it, remember this. Death before dishonour.'

Life was too sweet for Joe Burns. He had the kind of noble face that looked as though it had been chiselled out of a mountain; and wavy hair that was all his own, no chemicals applied. Joe was popular with women. 'Him a sweet bwoy,' they said but he was not a sweet-back who'd put up his feet and let a woman 'keep' him. His ways were a regular topic of conversation for my father and his spars. It was a risk, but I decided to venture on a little conversation with Bageye, spicing my comments with some of the things I had heard the big men say. What puzzled me about Joe Burns, I said to my father, what I really couldn't work out, was which of the two women Joe lived with was his wife. They were mother and daughter. But both were as big as each other. 'Plenty man would like be in Joe position,' is all Bageye would say on the matter. It was true, all the fellas admired Joe. The mother and daughter may have been on the plain side. They may have had big bellies and been a little too fond of cheap perfume, but at the time when Joe took up with them, none of the other fellas could even stand at the same bus stop with a white woman.

Joe and his women lived up at High Town in one of those houses where you went from street to front room in one step. Except, on this day, there were so many sacks in the front room that we could hardly squeeze in. Each room in the house was full of hemp sacks. The sacks were full of corn on the cob and the smell announced that they were just beginning to turn. Joe was a wheeler-dealer; he was a man who always knew a man who knew a man. Only one man liked to take chances more than Joe and that was Bageye. And when the time came to leave Joe's, I knew that even though we already had enough corn to last us a month, we'd not be leaving empty-handed; that each hand would be carrying another bag of stinking corn.

Somehow Bageye seemed able to see my mother's disbelief and disdain anticipated in my own face. 'Mek her stay there cuss her bad word,' Bageye said of his wife. 'I know a man, one of my spars, might can do something with this.' I foresaw a future of corn on the cob for breakfast, lunch and dinner, and though I never saw the money change hands, I reckoned there'd be no more discussion about the merits of a carpet over lino.

The business with Joe Burns was a bad sign. Bageye was in the mood now of the repentant drunk or gambler, suddenly struck by the ennobling idea of settling his debts. If it was his last night on earth Bageye would have to pay his dues – at least those he could afford.

We pulled up outside the Indian tobacco shop. Mr Maghar was actually from Uganda. But it didn't matter that each morning as a boy Mr Maghar had risen at 5 o'clock to feed the goats on the hills of Juba, he was still a clever Bombay Indian who'd sell a man one shoe, as far as my father and Uncle Darcus were concerned. But Bageye was also a practical man and if he had to swallow his pride and ask for credit from a tobacconist, it might as well be from the 'Cha-cha' man close to home. For the last week I'd been going, at my father's beckoning, to pick up his Embassy Number 1 and a box of matches from Mr Maghar. As the week progressed, I'd also taken to bringing back a little something for myself as a reward. The one bar of Cadbury's chocolate – just this once – had become a daily routine. I reflected now that it was a strange coincidence because last year it happened to my brother. His inability to stop rewarding himself had seemed beyond his control, as if he was possessed. And that time when Bageye found out, he had unbuckled his belt. He never liked to do it, so he said, took no pleasure from it, but: 'If pickney cyann' learn then they will feel – simple so.'

Before leaving me in the car, Bageye warned me, as he always did, not to touch anything. I nodded, but I wasn't really listening. My mind was fixed on the image of my father in conversation with Maghar, unsuspecting of the size of the bill he was about to receive. I held onto the faint hope that he, somehow, wouldn't notice – a hope that slipped away with every minute of his prolonged absence. It probably wasn't that long. It was like that time I was knocked off my bike and everything appeared to be going in slow motion. I forced myself not to look out of the car window but had no control over ears that strained to hear him returning, trying to work out the menace, the degree of violence in his footsteps. Something told me to run. But where to? I was paralysed by anxieties, each one more sickening than the last. And it was with some relief that I heard the driver's-side door open, followed by an unexpected silence.

Bageye took an Embassy Number 1 and pressed in the cigarette lighter on the dashboard. While he waited for it to heat up an idea seemed to come to him. When the lighter pinged he held it up. But, by the time he put it to the cigarette, the glow from the filament had dimmed, so that he had to press the lighter back into the socket on the dashboard once more. 'If you want sweet, why didn't you come to me and ask?' Bageye spoke suddenly but quietly. 'Wha'appen? You don't have tongue in your head?' It occurred to me that lately I'd been shedding a lot of tears in front of my father. The truth was I could hold out against anger and violence but was wrong-footed when confronted by gentleness and disappointment. '"Didn't the boy ask your permission?"' Bageye mimicked Mr Maghar. He snorted. 'Is so the man speak to me. "Didn't the boy ask your permission?" You don't hear the slur! I didn't bring up my pickney to take liberty. And no one's going to take liberty with my pickney.' It frightened me that my father was working himself up into a temper, talking about his number one son as if I wasn't sitting there right beside him in the front of the car.'It must have been Maghar's doing. Maghar who encouraged the boy to spend more and more. And when it gone too far now . . .' Bageye sucked on the idea. He took a Polo mint from a near-empty pack and cracked it between his teeth. 'Bet it wasn't even that many chocolate. Expec' one or two extra bar found dem way onto the list, right? Clever Mr Indian think he can use his brains 'pon me. You think I born yesterday? Is forty-eight years ago I born. Mek Maghar stay there lick him chops. Is finish, I finish with him tonight.'

Tomorrow, Bageye would change his tune. Tomorrow I would have to run and fetch ten Embassy Number 1 or a pack of Marlboro and some Rizlas. But tomorrow, from Mr Maghar, I also knew, there would be no fantastic tales of herding sheep on the hills of Juba. Tomorrow, the kindly shopkeeper would hand over the cigarettes in silence and coldly cut his eye after me as I left the shop.

Bageye counted what was left of the money. He stopped and bid me check it for him. Already the notes were few and starting to look grubby. 'Even if I'm down to my last penny, that floor gone cover tonight!' Bageye stressed a little too earnestly. 'But bwoy, we take a knock with this sweet business, might have to make do with the lino after all.' He folded the money back into his clip. 'Only one wage coming in and we have to make it stretch.' He counted out £30 and asked me to hold out my hand. 'Squeeze tight. It the lino money. Blood money.'

But if I concluded that we must now be heading to Bernard's, I needed to think again, because Bageye first had to run by Anxious so the two of them could share a smoke. Although 'share' might not have been the most appropriate word. My father liked to smoke in company but he shared a cigarette the way he shared a joke: it was mostly for his own pleasure. His wife might begrudge him the smoke when the cupboard was bare, but the cigarette was the one little pleasure Bageye had.

Superkings held much more tobacco than a normal

cigarette, and if Bageye could break one up, unpack it into a Rizla, add a little something to make it sweet, roll it again, then he could make it last a whole heap of time.

Though I'd heard Mum describe him as 'misery who likes company', Anxious lived alone. The truth was he just couldn't seem to hold down a woman, the fellas used to say.

Anxious admired the cigarette as he dragged on the last draw, and I got up on cue ready to leave. 'Settle back into your seat, man,' Bageye said languidly, 'the day long.' And winking at me, added: 'Let me have ten from that t'ing I give you.' I knew better than to hesitate and handed over £10 from the £30 left in my charge.

'Is your son that, Bageye? Him turn big man.' Anxious laid a fat palm on my head. 'So, you is Bageye son?' There was something improper, taunting, in the way he said it. I couldn't figure it out, nor did I understand why he never addressed me directly. 'The boy want something to eat?' It sounded like a threat. Anxious had only a vague memory of how to cook. One time someone had shown him how you could boil up pig-foot to make soup.

'You never hear the man ask you a question!'

It was never clear how Bageye could become irritated so suddenly. He was like an old wound. Knock it and it would flare up. At times, you could be forgiven for thinking he actually resented the fact that children needed food and water. But what he resented more was the thought of Anxious, however innocently, pointing this out. Bageye lifted the lid on the pot and looked in scornfully. 'What this t'ing need is a little somet'ing spice it up.'

'You don't see the cupboard empty, Bageye?'

'You don't have no sweetcorn?' asked my father. 'No sweetcorn, no yam and cassava, no callaloo, no nothing. Not a t'ing.' Bageye opened up a succession of bare cupboards filled only with crystallised cobwebs. 'I cyann' make no promise but there's a chance . . .' He broke off and checked his watch. 'Have to move quick time. What you say, Anxious? I know a man, one of my spars, can throw three or four sack of sweetcorn your way, and a sweet price.'

Anxious drew back his head the better to suggest surprise. 'Three or four sack!'

'We not dealing with loose change here, you dig?' said Bageye. 'You don't have to eat the whole t'ing. Tek what you need and sell it on, simple so.'

Anxious ran a fat furry tongue slowly along the cigarette paper. 'What am I going to do with three or four sack of sweetcorn? Not even one or two but three or four?'

'One or two then,' said Bageye. And with that Bageye swept me out of the chair towards the front door. Anxious shouted after us: 'That sweetcorn better be sweet, you hear, Bageye.'

No matter which way he turned on the route back to Joe Burns's, my father had to drive past Bernard's. He braked sharply outside the junk shop. We sat in silence as Bageye turned over the unwelcome thought that my presence had forced upon him: 'To buy or not to buy the lino.'

A bell rang as we stepped inside. We pushed past all the junk at the front of the shop to all the junk at the back. To the unsuspecting eye, Bernard looked like a grey and feeble matchstick man with a cigarette permanently glued to the side of his mouth. But though you might think he was unfit, his passion was karate. He was a black belt and famed as the only man in Luton ever to have made a citizen's arrest, when some light-fingered fool tried his luck in the shop. The poor man hadn't read the signs. Where other shopkeepers displayed the usual placards – '*In God We Trust, Everyone Else Pays Cash*' – Bernard had simply hung his embossed black-belt certificate on the wall behind the till. The citizen's arrest had made the headlines in the *Luton News* a few years back. Multiple copies of that edition had been used to wallpaper the shop. Together with the framed certificate, they put the more discerning customer on notice that he or she should beware the quality of the man behind the counter. Bernard held out rolls of lino for Bageye to choose from. Each one was worn thin, stained and cracked, and not much better than the one on the floor back at our house. My father was clearly affronted by the inferior quality of the lino Bernard had deemed fit to present to him.

'How much for that one there, on the top shelf?' he asked. Bernard gazed sceptically at my father.

'That one's nearly new.'

'That's not what I asked. Cho, man!' Bageye put out his hand and I passed him the remainder of the money. He slapped the twenty down on the counter. 'Hold this as deposit, nah, man. We soon come with the rest.'

Back in the car, Bageye invited me to reflect on the meaning behind the words 'That one's nearly new,' again and again. 'You see how the man speak to me! And in front of my pickney!' First Maghar and now

Bernard. My father was so vexed he could spit: 'I've been among these people long enough to know what strokes they play. Bwoy, it not a good idea to stay in white-man country too long.'

Outside Joe Burns's yard, my father kept the engine running. He went in and came out in a hurry, returning to the car with two more sacks of corn. Things were moving fast now. In half an hour Bernard's would be shut. We got back to Anxious in good time. Bageye rolled out of the front seat, leaving the car door open. 'Only one more stop after this, little man,' he assured me, and, for the briefest moment, I saw an expression on his face that I did not at first recognise. Bageye smiled. I swear, my father smiled at me. I told myself to hold onto the memory; to remember to tell the others.

Ten minutes passed before I saw him again. Bageye was not renowned for sharing whatever was on his mind, but it was all too easy to pick up the bad vibe as he approached from Anxious's place. Something had gone horribly wrong. And, if I wasn't mistaken, there were two more sacks of fermenting corn being shoved onto the back seat. Bageye had gone in with the two sacks he'd expected to sell, and returned with them. He almost broke off the car key when he turned the ignition. The deal with Anxious can't have gone to plan. The mood he was in now, never mind carpet, you could kiss even the cheapest piece of lino goodbye. 'You cyann' sit still!' my father barked at me even though I hadn't moved a muscle since he got back in. It was a very bad sign. Worse was that we were now heading for home.

Bageye didn't bother to knock; that wasn't his style.

With the sacks of corn in his arms, he struggled to open the front door. My mother retreated a little, stepped to one side, planted her feet and hissed: 'I'm not saying a word.' Bageye paid her no mind. He threw the sacks under the kitchen sink and hurried back towards the front door. 'What about the lino?' The words came despite her pledge, dripping in sarcasm. Bageye turned to his wife and let fly a stream of bad words. He cursed her and then cursed some more. And the curses remained in the air as the front door slammed shut after him.

Bluefoot

S ELMA NEVER WANTED STRAIGHT HAIR, only that it should be more manageable. Hair-straightening, after all, was a kind of torture. A copper comb and the flame from the gas stove were the instruments of torture. To straighten hair, to 'conk' it as our mum called it, with the hot copper comb, she needed the cool nerve of a fighter pilot and the steady hand of a brain surgeon. Tiny twirls of brown paper were used to tie the strands of straightened hair in tight bunches, and finally the cut-off foot from a stocking would be stretched over the singed hair. That she did Selma's hair almost every other Friday night was a marvel to us all. My eldest sister, of course, always seemed a little more ambivalent. She'd be pleased or relieved by the end result but often gave the impression that she'd been subjected to a criminal act.

Selma's hair wasn't what you'd call good hair. For one thing it was a little on the short side. More damaging still, it was forever dry. If some of us had fine hair, then, as our mother would often remind us, that was down to her side of the family. Bageye's people were country people. Hair-wise, you could say that my father's people were more James Brown than Smokey Robinson. Their hair was a triumph of science over nature. Proof that you could defy the curse of nature and didn't have to live with the hair you were born with.

Out of us five children, Bageye was most sharp towards Selma. I suspect when he looked at Selma, my father saw himself; my sister's hair a reminder of his country roots. The cruel truth was that you might leave Jamaica, travel over 3,000 miles and emigrate to England, but you couldn't disguise your past. To those who knew, like my mother, there was such a thing as 'breeding'. Wistfully, she would announce, for no apparent reason: 'My people never put basket 'pon dem head go market.'

My mother was especially skilled at uncovering those who tried to pass themselves off as something other than what they truly were. A kind of humorous scorn was reserved for a man or woman sporting 'wet-look' hair from chemicals that came out of a bottle. 'A man will have the "wet-look",' said my mother, 'his wife will have the horse-hair weave on down to she bottom. But put them together and the pickney will have the real thing!' It was a mystery to me, though, that her powers of detection must have failed each night she lay down with Bageye.

Watching my mother straightening Selma's hair was a frightening experience because one slip of the comb would have scorched her daughter's scalp – though in all the years of straightening she never did. All through this Friday-night ritual, Mum hummed a never-ending cycle of hymns. The copper comb clanked on the stove as it was turned and heated on both sides. Grease was slapped into palms and rubbed into the hair. Selma's hair sizzled. It had been two weeks now since the hair was last conked and in that time it had run riot.

There was a certain tension in the air which couldn't

be explained solely by the fear of an accident. The conversation usually descended into a call-and-response type of argument. Back and forth it went like some well-rehearsed comedy sketch underpinned with resentment. As far as Selma was concerned if Mum hadn't married Bageye then she wouldn't have been born with trashy hair. For her part, my mother never failed to point out that Selma was a 'real Grant', which is what Bageye's people were called, and just occasionally this woman, who it was clear deeply loved her children, would bring the argument to an end with the resounding: 'Girl-child? You should drown them at birth.'

As if the hair wasn't enough, on Fridays too there was the constant unease about the house money. Thursday was pay day but Bageye liked the feel of the fat wages, the full amount in his pocket, for one day at least before it all started to drip away. He handed over the 'house money' to my mother on Friday nights – sometimes. When the mood took him otherwise, then it was another story.

That moment, the window of opportunity, when there was still money about, was very short. Mum had coached us in how not to pass up this fleeting chance; to urge Bageye to do the right thing; to remind him of certain hard facts; to encourage him, for instance, to observe the seats of our pants that were shining through or to tune his ears to the flip-flop sound of the soles separating from the bottoms of our shoes. There was reluctance on all our parts to pass on this information, much to my mother's exasperation. 'Don't come cry to me when you grow too big for the overcoat and the cold wind cut your skin,' she would sigh.

She was absolutely right. The warm glow of contentedness would drain quickly from Bageye. Then we all waited for the click of the front door closing which announced that he had left the house. No one could quite bear the strain of his imminent departure and the sickening fear that he might change his mind. But my father liked to draw it out. Man, he was going to leave in his own sweet time. Living with Bageye was like living under enemy occupation; an enemy who had come to doubt the wisdom of the invasion but could see no honourable way to withdraw. I imagined, though, that we were just as much the enemy to him, and that he would always be outnumbered if not outgunned.

No matter how much overtime my father put in, the separate money Blossom had persuaded him to put aside for possible school fees never seemed to accumulate. We always had to dip into it. 'Quicksand' was Bageye's name for this makeshift school fund, and bwoy, how he regretted our mother ever talking him into it, suckering him into contributing towards an unnecessary luxury he could ill afford. What's more, it was looking as though we were all developing into 'real Adams all right!' He said 'Adams' – the name of my mother's people – as if something unpleasant had stuck in his throat. Bageye believed that the Adamses were bent on pushing him towards bankruptcy with their blind ambition and faith in education. He hadn't even had the privilege of finishing his schooling. Sure, Bageye wasn't educated but then, as my mother said: 'That man couldn't even pass worms.' And time and again she'd warn us about learning the real lesson of dangerous men like Bageye:

'A half-educated man is like a poisoner who knows everything about concocting poisons but don't bother come to him for the antidote.'

Bageye was not in the mood for Mum tonight. She had this way of not saying anything – of just looking, of cutting her eye after him – that could make his blood boil. He certainly was not in the mood to discuss the house money. Even so, I'd been volunteered to remind 'Satan' (my mother's favourite name for him) that if he was going out, we needed a 50-pence piece for the meter in case the electricity ran out. He was also to be briefed about Selma's needs; that she was due at a schoolfriend's party the next night, and that the one dress she owned had gone beyond a joke; you couldn't 'use it as rag to wash the floor'.

My father didn't want to hear any of this, naturally. From the spare room upstairs where he often slept before the night shift, the loud, pronounced clearing of the throat, the awkward snuffling and chomping sounds, could only mean he was building up to more immediate concerns. Right now, he made known as he trudged down the stairs, what was eating away at him, festering away, was the fact that 'someone leave the lid of the lavatory seat up!' Bageye wanted to know who did such a foul thing and he wanted to know now. 'You t'ink this is a joke t'ing?' he bellowed. He was deadly serious. The veins in his neck stood up. No one volunteered their guilt. We all knew that whether one of us made the miscalculation of putting up our hands, or no one did, there was still going to be hell to pay.

There was something of the perfectionist in my

father's attitude to life. The business with the toilet seat was merely an example of his very high standards. I didn't go along with Selma's theory that it came down to the fact that Bageye was 'a small man'. To me, he was like one of those crossword puzzles, where once you've figured out the code you would no longer be bamboozled. But though I was determined, in the summer of 1972, I was still a long way off from cracking the code.

Bageye seemed to teeter permanently on the edge of rage. We would not have been surprised to find one day that he had suffered spontaneous combustion, like the burning bush in the Bible. The previous week the poor man could barely contain himself because someone had left the lid of the lavatory seat down. Today, he was in a temper because the lavatory seat was up.

Struggling into his overcoat, mad arms caught up in sleeves that seemed too narrow, Bageye hoped we'd all, mother and children, got the message that he was not going to let us drag him down into the gutter. This was a difficult time for the poor troubled soul, a time when he was likely to lash out and leave you with a little somet'ing to remember him by. But as Bageye moved down the hallway, he caught sight of Baby G in the pram. And the clunk of the front-door lock closing, when it came, was like the trigger of the gun eased back into the safety position.

The relief was short-lived. Half an hour later we heard the dull click of the electricity meter without registering its importance quickly enough. The needle in the black box strained and swung back to zero and suddenly all the lights in the house went out. The orange glow from the filament of the electric fire held out for a while and then slowly faded to grey. Only the moonlight knocking at the kitchen window and the flame from the gas stove broke the darkness.

Mum issued her usual command: 'Nobody move.' It was more a refrain, lest her children fall down the stairs or bump into things in the dark. Carefully, balancing the hot copper comb on the stove, she checked the light switch for impossible signs of life, then felt her way to the box in the hallway housing the electricity meter. Our mother knew better than to expect a 50-pence piece sensibly placed on top of the meter but was still disappointed. No matter how hard she practised disappointment, she could never get it right. She would have to hunt throughout the house for another 50 pence.

There were several spots where she might have half hidden coins from herself just for this kind of emergency. At the bottom of the staircase, she knelt and ran a finger under the edge of the carpet but there was nothing there; it had been visited the night before.

Finally, she shouted: 'Where's the torch, little man?' as I knew she would. I bridled at the use of 'the torch'. It was not 'the torch'. It was my torch. I didn't answer but moved to where I knew the torch was hidden before it could be discovered. I heard her climbing the stairs, and Selma whispering: 'He's probably worried about the batteries.'

'Just a borrows till I find the fifty pence,' Mum said gently.

'I can't find it,' I lied.

'But who's going to buy him back the batteries

when they run out?' Selma mocked. My mother arrived at the landing and called upon God to give her strength. She entered the bedroom and pulled back the curtains to let some of the street light illuminate the room, and no doubt tapping into her extraordinary psychic powers reached down behind the immersion tank in the airing cupboard and pulled up the torch from where I had expertly hidden it.

Without involving me, a decision was reached quickly to dispatch me and Selma to Mrs Knight's gambling house again. Mum didn't like the idea of her pickney wandering the streets, she admitted, but she had no choice. We set off but as soon as we were out of sight we slowed, courtesy of an unspoken agreement, to an idler's pace of one foot in front of the other foot, from the toes of one foot to the heel of the other.

Thankfully, Bageye was nowhere to be found by the time we arrived. We were about to make our escape when one of the fellas, Castus, took pity on us and insisted on running us up to the hospital on Dunstable Road where he suspected Bageye had been heading – only suspecting, mind you. Bageye didn't usually work on a Friday night but the hospital was always good for a fare.

The quickest route to the hospital was along the old Roman road but Castus was convinced he knew a short cut. Not that he was in a hurry. I never saw a man who was more in love with the steering wheel; he just enjoyed turning it, preferably one-handed. The car was a marvel to him.

'How you like the way it hold the corners?' he asked. At times he sounded like Bageye.

Selma gave him one look – no more. Repeatedly she raised and lowered her legs. It was apparent that she was discomforted by the transparent plastic covers of the leather car seats which stuck to her thighs. The covers may have been there from new but were cracked in places and cut into your skin when you shifted your weight. Castus made a half-hearted attempt at an apology. He'd been meaning to change them for some time now. His eyes flicked up to the rear-view mirror, searching us out. He didn't bother to finish the sentence. Selma, I noticed, had become locked in that annoying silence of hers. Pretty soon it had infected the whole car.

No matter how hard you tried not to, your eyes were drawn to the rear-view mirror. And whenever you looked, you caught Castus's dead eyes staring back at you. Castus, it seemed, couldn't quite get over Selma's appearance, so intrigued was he by the edge of the stocking leg that he could just make out beneath her headscarf.

'You young gal start wear stocking early, eeeh?'

Castus was one of those leery old-timers with Guinness breath who was much less successful with women than he believed himself to be. I admired the way he cocked the trilby to the side of his head. He'd obviously watched a lot of early gangster movies in his time and tried for a style borrowed from them. He attempted the stocking-leg joke again. I smiled. Selma refused to. As soon as the car stopped outside the gates of the hospital, Selma yanked me out, with not even a thank-you for Castus. I didn't especially admire that.

She pushed me ahead of her: 'Just walk and don't look back.'

The night drizzle made the hospital buildings even gloomier. Except for the occasional crash of trolleys through swing doors, there was no sound. Selma had only been to the hospital once before but she walked with purpose, following the directions towards the jerry-built wards of the psychiatric wing where the minicabs tended to concentrate. If she was afraid, it didn't show.

I caught myself slowing down the closer we got. The dread was a familiar feeling. Like when it was your turn to climb the stairs and creep into Bageye's bedroom to wake him in time for the night shift. Your head said: 'Go on, you have to do it.' But your body had other ideas. The night-shift reveille would be nothing compared to the reception we could expect when we eventually caught up with him. I was all for turning back but Selma wouldn't have any of it. She dragged me along while I concentrated on the gravel underneath.

Bageye's car was almost hidden under the big sycamore tree. Though the cabin light was on, it was hard to make out his figure in the driving seat through the rain-spattered windows. Only a few yards away, we were overtaken by a woman – a nurse, I think – who in a few quick steps was round to the side of the car, pulling open the passenger door. She stubbed out a cigarette, blew the final puff through the gaps in her teeth, and kind of burped the way smokers do to get rid of their smoky breath. It was only then that she paused and glanced up at us; she looked a second time as if she knew who we were. Bageye wiped away the condensation from the windscreen the better to follow her gaze, and for the first time took in the sight of his miserable offspring. It was there in his eyes. He wound down the window and looked us over. 'The rass clat! She send the pickney spy on me now.' Bageye was taken aback by Selma's stockinged head.

'Is so you come out the street, so? You cyann' even mek yourself presentable! You have to come here, take me mek poppy show.'

Selma explained coolly, in her best elocutionist voice, that no one was trying to make a fool of him but that the electricity had run out and that he couldn't expect us to wait in the dark until it suited him to return. Selma had always been the bravest of us children. Ordinarily, she should have expected a sharp rebuke for speaking out, but for once my father faltered. The woman climbed into the passenger seat in the front and slammed the door behind her, harder than Bageye would have approved. My father rolled up the window and we heard them whispering to each other. Some agreement appeared to have been reached. Bageye's window rolled down. He rummaged through his pockets and counted out a few coins into Selma's outstretched hand. Selma was still holding out her hand as the window wound back up, the engine started and Bageye took off with his fare. Selma seemed excited suddenly.

'Well, well,' she said mischievously.

'What?'

'Oh, it's a funny business.'

'What?'

I had noticed recently that Selma had developed an annoying habit of weaving riddles and of treating

133

everyone, especially me, as an intellectual inferior. I suspect she thought it was funny.

'Didn't you see how she sat in the front with him?'

'So?'

'Passengers don't sit in the front seat.'

A few weeks ago, Bageye had fitted back seats for the extra fares. But it seemed reasonable to me that as you'd still have to lift the front seat to get into the back that you'd stay in the front if there was a choice. Selma disagreed strongly.

'Passengers don't sit in the front unless . . .'

'Unless what?'

'Unless they're not passengers. Get it? Don't you get it, stupid? That's her. Bluefoot Julie. What are you crying for?'

'I'm not.'

'Yes, you are.' Selma put on her sorry voice, although she would never say sorry. 'Why are you crying?'

Sometimes it was difficult to pick up on the things adults said. More often than not all you'd get was the tone. 'Bluefoot' was one of my mother's phrases. It came out when she couldn't take it no more, when she was vexed and unhappy with my father. A 'Bluefoot' was a nasty white woman. If not a prostitute, then close to it. The kind of white woman who never wore tights even in the cold and whose feet and ankles were subsequently blue. Suddenly, after several years, my mother's curses at Bageye on a Friday night made sense to me. Most Friday nights when he'd completed the delicate task of ironing his kerchief and checking the stiffness of the starched collar on his shirt before heading out the door, my mother would shout after him: 'Yes, go run to your bluefoot.'

Selma tried to involve me in a discussion about whether to tell Mum what we'd seen, but I couldn't even be sure what Bluefoot Julie looked like. Whatever happened, we knew that Bageye would be ready for us when he came through the front door the next morning; we were sure to be in for a fine old time.

Waiting for Bageye was always worse when you'd had time to sleep on it. The morning would come and there'd be no sign of him; 10 o'clock, nothing; 11 o'clock, nothing. There'd be a critical point, say 11.30, when you knew that if he hadn't shown by then, you could relax, he wouldn't be home for the rest of the day.

No one would admit it but everyone would be watching the clock. At times you got it horribly wrong, of course. Sometimes you found that Bageye had slipped into the spare room in the middle of the night or had fallen asleep on the settee in the front room. Then you'd only become aware of his presence when you heard the repeated angry flushing of the toilet upstairs.

If there was a routine to Saturday mornings then it was the frenzied campaign in damage limitation before Bageye's return: draw the curtains to cover any newly broken windows in the dining room; knock back the broken arm of the settee into position; shiny-shine the bathroom taps till you see your reflection in them; prop up the drop-down door; and toss a coin for the lavatory seat – heads up, tails down.

Not everyone entered into the Saturday-morning spirit. 'Might have to take a rain check.' Selma had only recently learnt the phrase. 'Put me down for a double shift next week, OK, guys?' She said this with a lazy New York twang, not lifting her head from the steady business of painting her nails with the blood-red varnish the Avon lady had left behind for a trial.

'Besides, I'm not afraid of the evil wretch.'

Of course she wasn't. Bad as he was – and he was bad – Bageye would never lift his hand to a girl-child.

Mum told us to stop our contention. She said it even before it began. Mum had been working through the night to knock out a simple party dress for Selma to wear to her friend's birthday do. And as far as I was concerned, Selma didn't struggle hard enough to hide her disappointment. She didn't like the quality of the fabric: everyone would know it was a cheap imitation. Sure, a finer material would be nice but as Mum explained: 'If I don't have it, then I just don't have it.'

Our mother was at pains to point out that we had to work together, that 'one finger cyann' crack lice', and, if God spared her life, next year Selma would have a proper party dress. But for now she would just have to make do.

Mum was interrupted by a thud, a low rumble coming through the ceiling. It was the unmistakable sound of someone flushing the lavatory. Nothing was said, but as if on cue, everyone assumed a busy stance, performing some suddenly vital chore, or watching the television intently. Bageye came slowly down the stairs, pulled open the dining room door and surveyed all that he was master of – his wife and his progeny. It was immediately clear that the demon that had entered his spirit last night was yet to leave him. He looked as though he'd just been paid the biggest insult of his life, as though fate was taunting him.

Mum worked the pedal on the sewing machine; its hum matched her own. But for a change Bageye didn't bother with her. It was Selma and me who came under scrutiny. He stared at us in such a peculiar way; it reminded me of the look Bluefoot Julie had given us last night. Selma spread out the fingers of both hands and blew her nails dry.

'Is where you gwan with dem claw?' said Bageye.

Mum pulled through the thread on the bobbin. 'She going to a friend party. The pickney must have some fun.'

'I talking to you? No, I talking to the gal. T'ink she turn big woman. Cho! I ask you again. Is where you gwan with dem claw? Is fling you would like fling dem claw in my face?'

Selma didn't bother to answer him. She brushed her fingers through the air. A year ago Selma wouldn't have been so casual, not even a month ago, but Selma knew and Bageye was beginning to, that she was growing into a big woman and couldn't be intimidated like the rest of us.

If that was what Selma thought then Bageye suggested that she think again. Because it didn't matter how big any of us children got, once Bageye made up his mind to do something, that's it. And he was going to prove just what he meant. Bageye pulled open and rummaged through the drawers of the sewing machine.

'You not leaving the house with dem claw, you understand.' He picked up a pair of scissors. 'Bring disgrace 'pon my head, take me mek poppy show. No, man!' Bageye got Selma in a kind of armlock. He unfolded her fingers from the fist she had made and started, clumsily, to cut her fingernails. Selma hissed at him: 'Why don't you go run to your bluefoot!'

She struggled for a while and then suddenly she kind of flopped; she didn't give in but offered no resistance. Hot with humiliation, her red eyes darted around the room. My mother screamed at Bageye, cursed him and we, brothers and sisters, as usual, averted our gaze.

This Here is Bush

'THIS HERE IS BUSH ALL right, real bush.' Mum looked hard at the four walls of the room and the walls stared right back at her. She looked away and by the time she looked round again the walls had crept forward, closing in on her. The walls mocked her. The house mocked her, as did the council estate. Less than a hundred yards away the constant drone of cars speeding on the M1 motorway sounded like jeering. Their occupants were on their way. She did not know where they were heading but they were most certainly not stuck in Luton – let's be honest, it was not even Luton but Farley Hill, on the edge of town: bush, in other words.

We had never been to Jamaica where both our parents were born but the word 'bush' produced a shudder in all of us children. 'Bush', we worked out, meant something dark and foreboding, and also shameful. 'Bush' places in Jamaica were unreachable by made-up roads and had pitiful names like Porus (Poor Us). Their dirt-poor inhabitants made do, just as the generation before them had, with kerosene lamps and pit toilets; the 'bush people' were plagued by swarms of mosquitoes as big as clouds, and walked about with machetes in hand to clear paths that were forever in danger of being reclaimed by the wild.

Even though we grasped the basic idea, I suspect

that my siblings, like me, were never entirely convinced that anywhere in our parents' homeland could be anything other than the idyllic island in the sun described by Harry Belafonte. 'Bush' was just one of hundreds of words and phrases both Bageye and Blossom spoke, almost as another language, that at times seemed impossible to translate. When we thought of bush, TV images of the jungle sprang to mind. Essentially, it was an African jungle that was home to the loinclothed, wavy-haired Tarzan who swung effortlessly through the trees and summoned the animals with his powerful jungle call. Or else it was grinning 'yes, boss' Africans from the TV show *Daktari* – although the jungle of 'Clarence the Cross-eyed Lion' never seemed to vary from week to week, no matter how hard the producers tried to disguise the Los Angeles studio set that it so obviously was. Bush, the pitiful and pestilent African interior, somehow had to be transplanted onto parts of Jamaica – that was the best we could do, the furthest our imaginations would take us.

But bush was also where bush people were to be found, and that's where the trouble really lay: you could take the person out of the bush but something of the bush always remained, something of the primitive. Bageye and Blossom might skirt around the subject but every now and then it slipped out. It was the source of much of the tension between them. Blossom's people were refined: they had good hair and a good colour. Black-and-white photos of them in snazzy double-breasted jackets and elegant floral dresses adorned the mantelpiece in the living room. Snapshots of Bageye's people, by contrast, had not made it onto the mantelpiece – or anywhere in the house. The reason was obvious though it wasn't often spoken, or if it was then not within earshot of Bageye. In my mother's estimation, Bageye's people – though not 100 per cent 'bush' – bore a closer resemblance to man's cousin than she was comfortable with. Or put another way, she didn't want 'no damn monkeys spoiling the photos on the mantelpiece'.

My father never spoke about his family. He never volunteered any information, and actually, though it seems odd now, none of us ever appeared to be curious. It was almost as if there was only ever Bageye and he took up so much space in all of our heads there was no room to think about anyone else, his brothers or sisters (if he had any) or his parents. Though it was never mentioned, you knew that such things ate away at him, like the ulcer which was barely relieved by a glass of milk. He never uttered the name of any relative (apart from Darcus) and when he called the names of Blossom's family it always came out as a kind of slur, as if the names stuck in his craw.

Perhaps snapshots of his family were tucked away in a wallet or in some document in his drawer but he never framed them for the picture rail or suggested them for the mantelpiece. And yet, every time he walked into the living room he was confronted by the sight of Blossom's family assuming pride of place in his house, on his mantelpiece.

One day I came home with Mum to find, unusually, the living-room door wide open. We walked into the room and Bageye was there waiting, with an elbow propped up on the mantelpiece, in the kind of pose a professional photographer might have directed. Only he wasn't at ease. It looked as though he'd been waiting for her to return for a very long time. He was extremely agitated, though his hands were perfectly still.

Between his fingers and thumbs he held one of the photographs of Blossom's relatives, and once he had his wife's full attention, he very, very slowly began to tear up the photo. On completion of that task he turned to the next photo. And one by one he proceeded to destroy each of those beautiful black-and-white snapshots that had – ever since I could remember – been dusted each week by Blossom and repositioned carefully on the mantelpiece, until they formed a carpet of confetti on the floor.

Mum never wept over this, as you might have imagined. Hours later she pointed out that she had 'done stop cry a long time ago'. Her fountain of tears had dried up over the years, and besides, 'What you is, is what you is,' she said. 'What else can you expect?' Bageye's vandalism was just confirmation, she maintained, of the 'evil wretch's stinking bush attitude'. Blossom's class of people would never have carried on so. And this was the danger. Living in the bush brought out the bush mentality. Bageye was no exception: 'You lie down in the gutter with dogs; you get up with fleas.' If ever she doubted that her husband was at heart a bush man then the business with the photos was the proof.

Life is what it is. Both our parents firmly believed this. I didn't notice any recognisable difference in their attitude towards each other in the following weeks. Bageye still ate first and alone at the dining table: a plate of yams, potatoes and rice on one side; and a plate of stew, curried goat or chicken on the other. Important matters were still discussed on a Saturday afternoon as they sat on the edge of the bed, at right angles to each other, staring out the window and into the future. You'd have thought they were only acquaintances but they were no cooler with each other than normal: there was never any intimacy between them, not even a fleeting holding of hands or an offer to straighten a tie or zip up the back of a dress. Perhaps it was this that contributed to the feeling, which none of us quite got over, that when our father was about there was a stranger in the house.

One morning I spied my mother coming up the stairs with a sheet and blanket. Nothing odd about that except it was about 7 a.m., before school preparations had even started, and too early for the washing to have been put on the line and dried. The same thing happened on the following day, and on the third. On the fourth day, I noticed that she was also carrying a pillow, and when I sneaked into the living room I saw that the settee was not its usual shape; the imprint that her body had made on the cushions had not yet faded. Obviously, Mum had moved downstairs, was sleeping apart from her husband in the living room, and had probably been doing so ever since the business with the pictures. She carried on with the charade for a day or two longer, and then dropped it altogether.

This was the time when you got a sense that there was some weird physics at play in the house. I used to think that the house was really two houses, or perhaps one house in two dimensions, that allowed us and our mother to move about in one plane, and our father in another – just as ghosts were said to be ever present but beyond our reach. Our parents occupied the same space but were not in the same space. You looked at Bageye and he appeared to have lost his colour and everything around him seemed out of focus, a little like the hazy effect you could get by squeezing your eyes tight shut and then opening them very quickly – grey dots suddenly swirled in front of you in an alluring otherworld. And you'd start to consider that maybe, just maybe, Blossom wasn't exaggerating. Maybe our father really was Satan.

After a month of this carrying on, the downstairs sleeping stopped abruptly one day. We woke to a scream from our mother, so terrifying that no one was willing to go down and investigate. The truth was only revealed a bit later when we scrambled down to breakfast: there was a bruise under Mum's right eye where the duppy (ghost) had slapped her.

The settee as bed was abandoned thereafter. Mum returned upstairs, even though I soon heard her complain to a friend: 'That man Grant only have me as a warming pan.' She was not happy, but resigned to it: there was nowhere to retreat to. Worse now, she was also permanently troubled, racked by the unsettling idea that there was a duppy at large in the house. Turning off the lights at night and bolting the front and back door didn't help because the duppy was on the inside. She warned us that she would have to get serious because: 'A duppy is not a easy somet'ing.' Ingenuity was called for. Last thing at night, she took to leaving a pair of scissors on the bottom step of the staircase, opened. She reasoned rightly, of course, that the duppy wouldn't climb the stairs and follow her up to the bedroom for fear of being wounded.

It made perfect sense to all of us, apart from Selma who always scoffed whenever the subject of the nightly ritual came up. One day I confronted her and she laughed at my naivety, and made up her mind right away to give it to me straight. According to Selma the scissors were left out for Bageye so Mum'd be able to hear when he sneaked back into the house, returning in the early hours after a night of gambling at Mrs Knight's. Catching himself on the scissors would also give him something to think about.

'No, the scissors are for the duppy,' I argued.

'What duppy?'

'The duppy that boxed her.'

'No duppy slapped her,' said Selma, smiling in that infuriating pretend-adult way of hers.

'What about the bruise then?' I asked triumphantly.

'Well, you know who gave her that particular present.'

'The duppy?'

'Don't be cute.' Selma kind of laughed and snorted at the same time, catching the tail end of the laugh before it finished. 'You know all too well . . .'

It wasn't always wise to stay in an argument with Selma. A lot of the time, you couldn't be sure what she actually believed in. She didn't believe in the bogeyman in the attic or the duppy downstairs. Both were something she called 'a figment of your imagination'. She even had the crazy idea that there was no such thing as God. I didn't mind her holding these strange ideas but it wasn't right that she enjoyed telling us them so much.

In the end, though, you had to pay attention to Selma because she was often the carrier of inside information. Occasionally you'd overhear her and Mum whispering together. Selma would probe and Blossom would tell her things that she never relayed to anyone else. Even when you could make out what was being said, it often made little sense. After the photo incident Selma asked Blossom why she had married Bageye in the first place, and Mum answered strangely by talking about chickens forced to eat scraps: 'Them pick it and them pick it until them pick fowl filt'.' I would only make the connection years later that she was talking about being so choosy that in the end she was left with no choice; at the time I hadn't a clue.

Mum would have left the house long before if she'd had an opportunity but really she had no alternative, for all our sakes, but to stick and stay. Though Bageye often remarked that we shouldn't grow too comfortable in England because it was 'nah good to stay in the white man country too long', Blossom knew her husband was bluffing: he never wanted to go back to the Jamaican bush. He was a man whose ambition had peaked with our arrival on the estate, and despite his protests, Blossom believed her husband to be right at home among the residents of Farley Hill. For, though she would never have addressed them as such, the small numbers of black folk on the estate were his kind of bush people. Please, you just had to look at their coarse hair. It didn't matter that they weren't from Jamaica. What went for our countrymen also applied to the 'smallees' from the smaller Caribbean islands – bush people whose patois was so distinct from that of the Jamaicans that we sometimes also called them 'language people'.

And it wasn't long before we realised that our English and Irish neighbours had their bush ways about them too: in their homes you were offered 'sugar water' to drink from sparkling glasses cleaned with spit and cloth, sometimes in your presence; you were served food from the same pot the Englishwomen used to boil their knickers.

Our mother was a very choosy person, but she could not have chosen to live in Farley Hill. Otherwise she would not have needed to ask herself as she repeatedly did: 'Is how I end up in this here bush place?' The thought of not just where but how we were living was enough to drive her mad. She wasn't the only one. Some of Blossom's friends, who had come from 'good homes' in Jamaica where they'd had respectable jobs, for instance as teachers, came to England and somehow ended up working on the factory floor at Vauxhall Motors. One or two had eventually returned to Jamaica but they were now not so stable in the head – not quite right. You could see it even before they left, and when I asked my mother what was wrong with them, she looked far off and said quietly and sadly: 'England mad them.'

Blossom wasn't going to let the same thing happen to her. One evening she sat down and worked out a plan. We didn't know at the time. The clue was in the back copies of the weekly *Jamaica Gleaner* we found in a kitchen drawer six months later. That was my drawer. I'd commandeered it (before any of the other kids got their hands on it) as a place to stash my *Beano* comics collection. There was never enough room to store all of our vital junk. Each of us had a hiding place; and it worked by everyone pretending not to know about the other person's. Up until then no one had stopped to think that our mother might consider herself to be in on the unofficial arrangement – until the discovery that my comics had been switched with the *Gleaner*. All of my *Beano*s were missing.

My mad overreaction – you'd have to call it a tantrum – took me by surprise because I'd been training to turn myself into stone, cold stone. The heat from my head was overwhelming, and I gave in to it. There was no excuse. I worked myself up into an enormous lather of emotion that I was loath to give a name to, never mind try to explain.

Afterwards, the *Beano*s were never mentioned again but the *Gleaner*s continued to pile up in the drawer she'd captured from me. One day I came home to find the latest *Gleaner* spread across the kitchen table. My mother pored over the pages with a pen poised in her hand – one of those tiny plastic biros Bageye used when he was studying the form of horses and marking up possible winners.

As far as I was concerned, we were still not on speaking terms. I knew this to be the case as I had initiated it, but I wasn't entirely sure that my mother understood just how deadly serious I was. It was difficult to convey without speaking, and that would have been out of the question.

'Come and have a look,' said Mum, beckoning me over.

'What are you doing?' I asked, surprising myself by how easily my vow of silence, just a few days after I had committed to it, had been broken.

'I'm looking about a piece of land,' said Blossom.

She turned to the back pages slowly and deftly with the assurance of a white-gloved librarian handling a rare text. My gaze followed her eyes which fell on the adverts for plots of land for sale in the Jamaican capital, Kingston. She ringed the possibilities, reading out the names. They sounded far off. There was a romance to the names: Red Hills, Constant Spring, Hope Pastures, Barbican Heights. These were all residential areas, she explained, lovingly rolling out the word: *residential*. Simply speaking the word seemed to give her enormous pleasure, so much so that I was almost jealous of it. If only there was something we kids could do to achieve such a transformation in her, no matter that it was only momentary.

On the final page there were a number of rough ink sketches of futuristic houses – some were two-storey but most were bungalows – all with flat concrete roofs. The price of each house was printed alongside. Mum, it transpired, had set her sights on one of these properties. She'd made up her mind. Though what she was going to use to buy the house was not clear. As if she could read my thoughts, she said in the dreamy voice that came out whenever she spoke of the past: 'Sometimes you have to make sacrifice. Take Arlene now . . .' Mum launched into one of her favourite tales. We never tired of these stories because, no matter how familiar they were, we could rarely work out conclusively their meaning or moral – though we knew there had to be one in there somewhere: it was often, vaguely, something to do with 'coming down in life'.

'You remember I told you about Arlene?'

'Who's Arlene again?' I asked. I don't know why I pretended to be ignorant (it drove a rivet into the edifice my brothers and sisters had built up of me as a fake), but there you are.

'Jus' a little topsy gal,' said Blossom. 'She used to run errand for my mother. Well, one day – must have been six months after Arlene stop work for us – she came to the back of the house bawling on account of she had gone for a job as a tailor assistant and she never get it. She was too dark for the tailor.' Blossom explained how her own mother had chastised Arlene, and that what she had to say to the girl had stayed with her all her life.

'If you cyann' get the job to cut the cloth, you must can get a job to wash it.'

Blossom said no more. When I asked her what it meant, she merely repeated the phrase with added emphasis, as you would for someone who was hard of hearing. I felt there was more to the story, but she didn't want to go on with it. She returned to the newspaper, to the plots of land and the developers' drawings for the new homes. She took time to explain to me how the diagrams for each house revealed the true layout of rooms; how the building would be designed to take account of the rising and setting of the sun so that the cooler back rooms were nearly always in the shade; how the kitchen connected with the larder and all the children's bedrooms with each other. She asked whether I could imagine living there, in such a house. I could. In fact, everything made sense apart from one room which she called the 'servant room'.

'Servant room?'

'That's right.'

'Who will live in the servant room?'

'But nah servant gwan live there. Who else?'

What she said made no sense. Television had informed me, my brothers and sisters that servants were in the paid employ of aristocrats, quartered in the attics of elegant Georgian homes and forever dressed in pinafores. Did she, I wanted to know, have servants when she lived in Jamaica, really?

'But nah must,' answered Mum. 'What I just tell you about Arlene? Everyone had servant.'

'Arlene was your servant?'

'Was,' Blossom answered pointedly. 'Was!'

That our mother had servants was as difficult to imagine as my father emerging from the Jamaican bush. But it was true. Blossom's people had always had a domestic help or a maid – somebody's cousin come from the country, usually, and in need of work. You had to train them up, of course, or before you knew what was what they had 'turned the house upside down'.

Mum returned to the story she'd broken off from telling me earlier. I hadn't previously heard the tale told in such detail. It required much concentration. Arlene, she said, had never had 'much polish, and she was facety too, so she didn't last long'. One time when Blossom was about fifteen, she had spotted Arlene on the street in downtown Kingston, and realised immediately there was something not quite right about her: Arlene was in her maid's uniform but without her maid's hat. 'It was a big disgrace, as you can imagine,' said Blossom. I nodded reflectively – the way the patient nods or smiles at the doctor when he gives them bad news – but could not imagine, not really. When Arlene returned home Blossom had arranged for her to be sacked. But if now, a lifetime later, Blossom was shocked by her youthful actions, she never let on. She just shrugged before I could make any comment: 'That's how life go.'

Tantalisingly, there was always spare money at 42 Castlecroft Road but it was locked away in meters – the gas meter under the stairs, the electricity meter in the alcove where coats were hung and the television meter. Tampering with the gas and electricity meters was useless. It should, however, have been possible to break into the television meter but we hadn't yet learnt the technique of sliding a kitchen knife back and forth into the slit on the coin box attached to the television. The rented Rediffusion set took 50-pence pieces and soon filled up. The sour man who came to empty the box every other week had set the meter to a higher rate than was needed. Mum explained that liberating a few coins would just be getting the rebate earlier than Rediffusion intended. But each time a coin was fed in at the back of the TV it dropped and settled horizontally on all the others. Blossom carefully pushed a knife through the slit in the base of the coin box but no matter how hard she tried she couldn't work the coins into an upright position for them to be eased through the slit. Nobody could.

She gave up, retired to the kitchen and put a big pan of water to heat on the stove – a signal that hot-water bottles were about to be filled. Even though it was only just past 6 o'clock we were commanded to hurry up to the bedroom and into our bedclothes while we could still benefit from the 'little juice lef' in the light bulb'. Nobody was convinced that there was any real danger of the electricity running out, but as she spoke the bulbs appeared to weaken and lose life.

Though the positioning of the hot-water bottle was key and the closeness of your feet to it was essential if it was to have the remotest chance of taking away some of the chill from the icy sheets, the danger of missing out on the warmth didn't stop us from constantly scrambling in and out of the bed, or call a halt to the caravan of traffic from the bedroom to the bathroom and occasionally even down to the kitchen. On most early-to-bed nights Blossom had a regular appointment with frustration if not exasperation, but this night, having retreated to her bedroom, she did not emerge. It was odd enough to be worth investigating.

Selma appointed herself chief snoop and, peering through the crack in the door to our parents' room, whispered back the news that Blossom had reached under the bed and pulled out the cardboard dress box, the one with camphor mothballs. Mum, she said, was holding up the 'dressing-up dress' that we'd only seen her wearing from photos back when Selma was her only child and barely reached above Mum's knees.

'What is she doing now?' somebody asked.

'Stroking it.'

Selma silenced our chortles with the announcement that Mum was about to put on the dress. She reckoned Blossom was trying it on for size, determining where she'd have to 'let it out'. But even after giving birth to five children her figure held and aside from being a little tight in the sleeves, the dress was a perfect fit. There was no need for Selma to report any more because by now we'd all joined her at the bedroom door to witness Mum smiling but also wiping away tears as she talked to her reflection in the dressing-table mirror.

Speaking to yourself was something we associated with Bageye, but Blossom was equally prone to it. Whereas Bageye was given, in his speech, to lashing out at imaginary foes, Blossom had a tendency to berate herself. Her chest would heave as if something inside were trying to escape and had to be kept down. She would grow near tearful (never fully so) and angrily predict a desperate future. She was definitely 'gwan end up in the almshouse, just like Granny Reid'. She knew it. Actually, she might as well be in an almshouse because 'the man Grant' had brought her to the bush. We lost count of the number of times she asked: 'Is how I end up in this here bush place?' But on each occasion it was as if she was asking herself the question for the first time. She seemed genuinely and deeply surprised.

The joke was that although our mother considered herself something of a psychic, she had not foreseen – back in Jamaica when she hitched her fortunes to Bageye – that she would end up staring at the four walls of the house at Farley Hill.

After the dress, the shoes – with stiletto heels – came out of the box. They were more of a squeeze than the dress: once they were on they were on. And finally a felt half-moon hat, like something out of the roaring twenties, was pinned to her hair with grips.

She clasped shut a clutch handbag. None of us could be sure what any of it meant. Blossom stood for ever on the spot. She did not betray what she was thinking.

Milton had been wrapping an elastic band around his finger an impossible number of times. The blood began to drain from the digit but he could not now remove the band. He rushed into the bedroom and held out his finger for Blossom to do something about. She took a pair of scissors and as she carefully snipped the band to free his finger, Milton blurted out: 'Don't leave us, Mum.' We must all have harboured the same thought because each of us, apart from Selma of course, said something similar. And then, almost inevitably, the crying began. I was not immune to it. In fact, it was impossible to say who'd started it off. I like to think it wasn't me but it could have been.

The scene of utter devastation brought out the biggest smile on Blossom's face that anyone could remember.

'But I'm not going anywhere,' she laughed. Pretty soon we were all joining her and even outdoing her in our jollification. It went on for ever. Nobody wanted it to die down but it did. It dribbled away like a guest who had outstayed his welcome. In the beginning of this new silence, Mum turned not so much towards the window but away from us and said quietly: 'Where can I go?' She stayed with her back to us for a very long time. Eventually, she took a deep diver's breath and spun round, beaming bravely. She started to bark and we squealed as she chased us, her sheep, out of the room, until we were corralled in our own bedroom. When we were all in and under the blankets she pulled them tight and tucked them under the mattress, trapping us in bed. We were warned not to answer the front door to anyone and told not to worry as she would 'soon come'.

Our mother, like all West Indians (apart from the ones who worked there, I suppose), was afraid of hospitals. Whenever the conversation came up she'd explain: 'I scared of knife.' She feared the surgical wards most of all but felt she must pay a visit to Summer Wear who was still languishing on one of them up at the L&D. It was important she went, because no one had been to see him since the first week. By showing her face she would make sure that they, the surgeons and physicians, would be afraid to carry out any experiments on him – an anxiety she shared with Bageye and the fellas. Anyway, she wouldn't be long. Only when she'd turned off all the electrics and was certain that we had not only understood and were able to recite the instructions backwards, but also that we believed in what she had said, did she issue a set of instructions to Selma, none of which we could hear, and then she was gone.

The slam of the front door – sharp and final – had hardly petered out before it was replaced by the hiss of Selma letting out some of the secrets Mum had just filled her head with. And, just as with a punctured tyre you didn't know where the hiss was coming from, we didn't know why she was saying all these things. It might have been that she didn't know herself. Her first revelation, and her only one, was that there was more to the hospital visit than our mother had let on. Apparently, Blossom was going to 'kill two birds with one stone', Selma informed us, and apply for a job there as well.

'What as?' I asked.

'I've already said too much,' said Selma. And no matter how hard we pressed and even pleaded, she refused to say more.

Within the hour we'd all dropped off to sleep. Some time later – I don't know how long had passed – I was woken by the sound of Selma sliding out of bed and tiptoeing from the room. I waited a bit, then followed, keeping my distance and staying out of sight, as she joined Mum in the kitchen and pulled up a stool beside her at the table. I sneaked into the coat area close to the kitchen from where I'd be able to hear everything. The story came out in a flood with Selma hardly saying anything at all.

The hospital visit had not gone well. Blossom first sought out the domestic supervisor. When she found her, sitting at a desk in a small room crammed with lockers, Mum didn't know how to say what she wanted: she had never worked before. She also worried over a broken heel that forced her to stand more formally to attention than was warranted. Blossom ended up asking the woman whether she had 'a position'. The supervisor, she noticed, had big hands and thick fingers reddened perhaps from years of being dipped in hot water, in detergents and other cleaning chemicals. Blossom surprised herself by suddenly announcing into the silence that she was prepared to work with her hands. The supervisor looked up, lingering over Blossom's once fine and presentable dress clothes, but studiously avoiding her feet.

'You do realise, don't you, it's mostly cleaning floors, emptying sluice-buckets, that sort of thing?'

Mum said she nodded but the supervisor looked unconvinced. 'She must have realised I wasn't the type of woman who'd ever carried pan of water 'pon my head.'

The supervisor had brought the interview to an end with the words: 'I don't think you're cut out for this kind of work.'

'Then, of course, I start my crying,' said Mum. 'And the supervisor gave me some money so I could get a bus back home. As I was leaving the hospital, this ward sister, a black woman, was coming my way, I suppose to start her shift. She stopped right in front of me. Who do you think it was?'

Blossom didn't wait for an answer.

'It was Arlene. The same little topsy gal I told you about. She a matron in the hospital. Arlene!'

Mum pulled back from a wave of tears that were coming, coming, coming with the memory of the encounter.

'Of course she recognised me straight away even though we hadn't seen each other for twenty years. Arlene asked me what I was doing, and I told her. And she was shocked. I know she was shocked because she told me so, more than once. "Cleaning floors at the hospital? Are you mad?" She really thought I was mad. "Suppose that news ever reach Jamaica."'

Before Blossom found the bus stop she turned around and headed back to the hospital. She'd forgotten about seeing Summer Wear. When she reached the ward, though, she found the grey curtains pulled round his bay and the bed empty. She couldn't see any nurses so she asked the other patients where they'd taken Summer Wear, and not one of the patients would answer. It was obvious. How could she not know? Before the truth leapt from my lips, as I feared it would, I resolved to creep back up the stairs to bed.

I don't remember Blossom or anyone admitting that Summer Wear had not recovered from his fever. I thought about it for a while the next day, only for a little while, though. For that morning there was also a miracle which more fully captured my attention. Mum looked in on us in the dining room and caught my eye – the way she did when she wanted you to run an errand. By the time I got round to answering her silent summons she was no longer in the kitchen. The floor had been mopped and the detritus of breakfast put away. It was that tiny moment in the week that I always loved when everything was in order before the chaos spilt out again. So it was a bit of a niggle to see that she'd forgotten to shut one of the drawers. I tiptoed over to close it. It was the drawer where she'd lately been keeping the *Gleaner*. You had to pull it open fully before you could close it, and in so doing I was struck by the revelation that there was not one copy of the paper in sight. In their place was my collection of *Beano* comics – every single one had been returned.

A College Man

'IT'S NOT YOUR SUIT. IT'S the boy suit. Imagine a man wearing a child's suit! From I born, me never hear-a such a t'ing.'

Blossom was adamant that she would not give in to Bageye's demands that he borrow my suit. The roiling argument booming through the walls made me nervous. I had just put on the suit. Blossom had only recently finished paying for my and Milton's matching suits. They were tailor-made by Mr Donby, and she'd had to use all her charm to persuade him to extend the credit line that had already been exhausted. We'd only worn them once, to church, for my First Communion. Now their next outing was to be for an even more special occasion: the entrance exam for the private school where Mum dreamt of enrolling both of us. But there was a catch. Bageye's suit had been 'captured' by the dry cleaners in lieu of an outstanding payment on another item. He had nothing to wear.

Blossom accused her husband of making up the story about the dry cleaners. Really, he resented the fact, she said, that his sons' suits were better quality than his own. At this Bageye left the argument. We could hear him coming towards us. Milton scrambled into the cupboard. There wasn't enough room for both of us. Bageye entered before I'd found an alternative hiding place.

'Look. Look at me. Look at me.'

I turned towards Bageye as commanded.

'No matter how big you get, you will never look down on me. You hear me? You hear what I say? Never!'

Bageye wondered whether he needed to say it again. I assured him that he needn't – or rather my head did. I tried out a range of nods before settling on one that was perhaps a little clumsy and more of a bow. I suppose I bowed not just for me but also for Mum who'd caused his distemper. I'd have bowed even lower, prostrated myself like the priest in front of the altar, if needed. It was best not to chance the gesture being missed; best to leave no room for doubt. Ordinarily, our father shouldn't have had to remind any one of us of the respect that was due to him but, as he pointed out, directing his comments at his wife who no doubt was listening hard on the other side of the wall in the adjoining room: 'Some people is bad-minded. Dem poison the well, and the pickney drink from the well. And remember, that well cyann' run dry for now.' His eyes locked on me: 'Your mother give you a drink, what you gwan do?'

'Drink it,' I answered.

'Of course you gwan drink it. You nah gwan say, "Well, hold on a minute, super, dis look like poison."'

My father's height still exceeded mine by two inches but the business with the suit was bringing home the fact that the situation wouldn't remain like that for too much longer now.

'You mind if I borrow the suit? Just a borrows, you understan'. How much wear it get so far? One more time not gwan hurt.'

Mum had told Milton and me to put on our tweed suits for the exam. It was an entrance exam, so we had to make a good impression. That was her reasoning. The exam didn't just start when the examiner laid the paper on the table in front of you; it started well before. But there was a problem. Bageye would be accompanying his sons to the private school for the test but his suit was at the dry cleaners, and the laundry man 'don't play the game right', explained Bageye. Our father had paid for the suit to be cleaned but when he turned up to collect it the laundry man had surrendered the curtains that had been in the cleaners for months now, and kept hold of the suit. It couldn't be retrieved. None of this mattered, said Bageye, as far as what now needed to be done. I could see his position, couldn't I? When it came to it, wasn't it more important that he made a good impression with the school and the headmaster? 'Show me the father,' said Bageye, 'and I will show you the son, nah must.' As a matter of fact, he'd been thinking anyway, he said, that it might actually be better if I wore my school uniform.

'You wouldn't begrudge your father a borrows of the suit?' Bageye asked again, helping me off with the jacket. 'Is so family must stay.' He tried on the jacket. It was a little short in the sleeves but he'd been expecting that. Fortunately, Mr Donby, the tailor, had made the suit with extra material – the cuffs turned up – to allow room for growth. Bageye was ready with the nail scissors to let out the sleeves. He carried out the same trick with the trousers, extending them by a couple of inches. There wasn't time to iron out the creases. We were already running late. Once both his legs were in, Bageye pulled on the waistband and kind of jumped into the trousers, breathing in a little at the very end to fasten the button.

'They fit good,' he said, smiling. 'Don't you worry, them can fix up again.' I changed into my school uniform but must not have looked enthusiastic enough about the swap because Bageye added, sharply: 'If you don't feel for lend it, tell me now, you know. I won't ask you again.'

In truth, we all spent so much time trying not to display any emotion in front of our father that it often backfired, sometimes spectacularly. Rather than being disappointed, I was relieved about the suit. Despite the expense, the tweed was coarse, stiff and lifeless. The heaviness of the jacket pressed down on your chest making it difficult to breathe. The collar chafed the back of your neck. After five minutes – no matter even if it was winter – you started to sweat. Just the thought of putting it on made me perspire. But the most annoying thing about the suit was that Milton (whose own suit was identical) never complained. In fact, he called me a sissy every time I rolled my shoulders and tried to loosen the grip that the suit had on me.

A neutral observer would have conceded that Bageye carried it off. The man knew how to wear a suit. It was as if his small but perfectly proportioned body was built for it. The suit looked better on my father. Bageye would not have disagreed. He stood in front of the wardrobe mirror, and saw what his wife had suspected all those years ago when they'd first met, that he was damn good-looking. Next door, fifteen years on, Blossom could now be heard muttering a little too clearly: 'You pick it and you pick it till you pick fowl filt'.'

She was still continuing with her monologue as she descended the stairs to heat through the dinner she'd prepared earlier because it would be too late when we returned from the exam. It was fish – a rare treat. Our mother called it 'brain food'. All week she'd been talking about the virtues of 'brain food' which would help us get through the exam. And all week long she and Bageye had wrangled over the necessity of having fish. Blossom wouldn't budge. At one point Bageye had grudgingly suggested that the money situation might stretch to snapper, but even that had been hotly rejected by Blossom as snapper was 'more bone than anything else', certainly more bone than flesh.

Towards the end of the week it had leaked out that it wasn't really the fish that troubled him. The fish was only a symptom of some larger concern. He hadn't wanted to be the first one to say it but, with only one wage coming in, while the fish was folly, the idea of sending the 'two boy go private school' was madness.

'Me not even bother answer you,' said Mum, answering her husband. 'I gwan put them in. You can tek them out.' She had made up her mind that we'd be starting the school. If at some later date Bageye wanted to take us out that was up to him and his conscience – and his conscience, she predicted, would kill him – but for now the two boys were definitely going to St Columba's College.

'If dem pass the exam. You forget.' Bageye smiled. 'Dem have to pass the entrance exam first.' It probably came out more coldly than he intended. His smile broadened into an expression that was located somewhere between self-justification and apology.

'Oh, them gwan pass all right,' said Mum, serving out the snapper onto the plates. Her husband's dish was first, of course. Despite herself, as Bageye made to cut into the fish, she warned him: 'Watch out for bone.'

No matter how hard I willed it, my father could not see or recognise these small, spontaneous moments of tenderness on the part of his wife. Perhaps he chose not to. But I also imagined that at night, lying on his back, reflecting as I did on how each day had turned out, he rued the chance to act on those fleeting opportunities. He gave the impression of a man who was always thinking, yet there was a recklessness about him that was never far from sight.

We were clearing away our plates when there was a knock at the door. Blossom dried her hands and went quickly to answer before anyone else had a chance. A man in a grey overall stood at the doorstep, balancing a number of cardboard boxes in his hands, piled up so high we could barely see his face. It might just as well have been a biblical vision as far as Blossom was concerned. For a moment it appeared that she might drop to her knees, as she cried out: 'Yes, Lord, thank you, Jesus! Thank you!'

The delivery man was from the hat factory, and any resemblance to an archangel was accidental. He was gruff and mechanical. Depositing the first three or four boxes, he returned to the van and brought in the next load, and the next, forcing us to jump to the side as the hallway filled up.

Finally, he held out a form for Blossom to sign and, smiling, declined to answer her when she asked about instructions. She tried again. He took back the pen slowly, smiled once more and pursed his lips as if to whistle.

'Not my department, missus.' He turned and walked back to the van. 'Try looking inside.'

Ignoring her husband's protests, Blossom began shoving the boxes into the living room. Inside each box were a dozen hats, glue and a number of loose feathers. Mother's task was to prettify all the hats with the feathers. She'd receive 25 pence per hat, and her husband could stop all his contention, she said, because the hat money, together with the family allowance that Blossom had been saving for months now, guaranteed that there'd be enough to make a down payment on the school fees.

But rather than bringing Bageye pleasure, the news opened up a new avenue of attack from him about 'the book'. Where was the family allowance book? He demanded to know how much she had saved up. By rights, as it was his house, he should take charge of the family allowance. Where was the book?

Luckily, Joe Burns swung by the house before the argument could really get going. He pulled up in a lorry which looked new, but even I could tell that there was something wrong with the engine because it continued to creak and judder long after the vehicle had come to a halt and Joe had clambered from the cabin.

Joe was loose. Loose-limbed. Loose as a big cat. Just plain loose. Nothing troubled him. He was a man, Bageye used to say, who behaved 'as if him always on holiday'. Joe came into the house, tiptoeing through the obstacle course of hat boxes, and emerged into the kitchen like a boxer entering the ring, rolling his shoulders, jabbing the air. He invited Milton and me to throw a punch into his stomach.

'Give me all you got now, everything. I want you to lay me out.' Our punches were no more powerful than a gnat's but he reeled away, bouncing off the wall, as if he were about to go down for the count. He wrapped us up in his big arms to prevent further punches, and pulled out a coin for each of us from behind our ears.

His laugh seemed all the more pronounced alongside Bageye's silence. Joe extended his hand but Bageye refused it. Instead he gave Joe a long, disapproving stare. As his eyes travelled down, clocking Joe's tie-less shirt, jeans and Dr Martens boots, Bageye appeared to wince.

'Never have time to change,' pleaded Joe.

'Should-a mek time.'

'You fuss too much, man,' Joe shrugged. 'How the wheels?'

'The wheels is the wheels. Why you ask?'

'We have a little problem with the lorry.' Joe spoke slowly now, spelling out and giving space to the individual words.

'A problem?'

'Not a problem as such,' said Joe. 'More of a situation.'

'Is wha' you say?'

'The radiator. Man, look like the radiator have a crack. Cyann' fix for now.'

'Rock stone!'

Bageye rarely swore in the conventional way, at least not in front of his children. Instead he drew on an array of odd words and expressions – unique to him – that carried the message well enough. 'Farley's plum!' was another favourite but somewhat milder, denoting an unexpected setback not quite disastrous – lost keys perhaps or the unwelcome sighting of a forgotten creditor. An accidental hammering of a finger instead of a tack merited a 'Chirachilli'. But 'Rock stone!' only came out when Bageye was in a bind, and there was no obvious way out: he'd have to take the hit, not quite on the chin but roll with the punch and hope for the best. Though he said 'Rock stone', in its intensity it came out as if it was really more a case of 'Farley's plum' or even 'Chirachilli'.

'If it so, then it so,' said Bageye, removing his jacket.

Mum advised Bageye to leave his jacket on. It wasn't like him to give up so easily. She pleaded with him. When he started to undo his tie, her tone darkened. She spoke freely and sharply, even though Joe was present, in such a way that there was bound to be some reckoning with Bageye later on. She didn't care. Too much was at stake. She would not hold her tongue. Finally, she questioned her husband's commitment to his children's education and welfare: 'On account-a the man nah even pass worms, he nah want the pickney to achieve anything.'

'You nah hear what Joe say?' Bageye snapped. 'Radiator have a crack.'

'What about the Mini?' She directed the question to Joe.

'That car not starting for now,' answered Bageye. 'You have lead, Joe?'

168

Joe shook his head. 'But we can try a hill start.'

Bageye kept quiet. He looked over at his wife and then at Joe, seeming to weigh their roles in this newly fashioned conspiracy. Both vexed him but it was obvious with whom he was angriest.

'I not finish with you yet!' he barked at Blossom, fastening the knot on his tie once more, as he moved towards the front door. He held the door open and shouted back at us: 'Come if you coming!'

Joe moved instinctively towards the driver's-side door and held out his hands for the keys. For the first time in a long while we heard Bageye laugh – actually it was more of a chuckle.

'You mus' a-joke. T'ink me gwan let you mash up my wheels too? Listen, Joe, I stop joke longtime.'

'But this is not a joke-joke t'ing, you know, Bageye,' said Joe, taking up position at the back of the car. 'We only have one chance. If the t'ing don't start when we get to the bottom of the hill, this is one man nah gwan push it back up.'

Despite his words it was noticeable how little resistance Joe gave to my father. When he put his mind to it, Bageye understood how to command men. He intuited that, at some level, the fellas liked to be ordered about and to be given the chance to obey. Come crunch time this is the way it would always be: Joe pushing from the back and Bageye at the wheel.

Even though the handbrake was pulled taut, two bricks were always placed under the rear wheels to prevent the car from rolling away. Milton and I took up positions beside Joe. Crouching down at the wheels, we were instructed to wait for the signal to remove the bricks, at which point we'd then have to push for God Almighty. But before we began Joe had one last plea to Bageye not to jump in before the car had gathered sufficient speed.

Bageye wound down the window on the driver's door. He intended to push on the frame with one hand and steer with the other. Copying Joe, we put our shoulders to the back of the car. The slope in the road was gentler than we imagined, and at first, defying the laws of physics, the car would not budge. Eventually the wheels began to turn. We moved at jogging pace and sooner than expected the car's speed was in danger of exceeding our own: we could barely keep up. Bageye struggled to open the door. He glanced back but there was no panic on his face. For an instant, he was transformed into a racing-car driver. His corduroy cap became a leather helmet and the tight woollen suit was replaced by a boiler suit. We were the team pushing off our man from the stand and he rushing to jump into the racing car before it took off without him. And he did it. He scrambled in, turned the key in the ignition and the engine burst into life. The car accelerated down the hill.

Though no one spoke, I knew that each of us was overcome with a feeling of elation. We had that wonderful lucid moment few are privileged to share; of understanding that from now on everything would be OK. Here and now, and in the future. We would get to St Albans; pass the entrance exam at St Columba's College; stand on the podium on graduation day in our scholars' gowns at university while our proud parents dabbed away tears of exhilaration; and go on to become doctors or lawyers. We would prevail.

I could not recall being happier. We raced after the Mini. Even before we reached Bageye it was obvious that the car had stalled.

Like an athlete who realises that the race is lost, Joe pulled up and slowed almost to a stop a few yards from the car. As much as he wanted to, Joe would not be able to walk away, even though his face betrayed the thought that we wouldn't now be in this predicament if Bageye hadn't been so vain and stubborn in denying Joe (the much more experienced driver, after all) the glory of being the one to jump into the driver's seat as it thundered down the hill.

'That piss car not moving for now.'

No sooner had the words escaped Joe's lips than Bageye tried the key in the ignition, once more for luck. Miraculously, it started. Before the car could change its mind we set off with Milton and me in the back. Joe sat up front in the passenger seat, holding his tongue when he'd rather be holding the steering wheel. Ordinarily, Bageye and Joe got on like 'batty and chamber'. In fact, Blossom often used to screw up her face and wonder aloud, asking no one in particular: 'Me nah know what them find to chat about, do you?' But they weren't so chatty-chatty now. Neither man seemed to want – or perhaps be able – to break the spell of silence that had been cast, although Joe came close to speaking whenever we approached traffic lights. Bageye was so anxious to avoid missing the red light, so as not to have to stop and potentially stall again, that whenever a traffic light loomed into view he did some weird driving manoeuvre. The car went into a kind of free-wheeling, beyond-anyone's-control mode, where a crash seemed inevitable. Only once we were through the lights did Joe's background shuffling cease and he settled back into pure silence.

The road to St Albans first led to Harpenden – an upper-crust village with a florist, family butcher and baker. Though it was only five miles away we'd never been to Harpenden. We had to slow down when we reached the outskirts because that's how everyone drove: slow and respectful. Everything about the place, especially its look, was softer than Luton. The houses (set back from the road) were fringed by high hedges. Many of the men wore suits. They looked as though they wore suits every day. I had heard about them before. They were called commuters but I had no idea, at that time, of the meaning of this strange word. Apart from the commuters, people didn't seem to be walking purposefully on the streets but to be strolling. Elsewhere they were casually filling up their cars with groceries. The cars weren't the Luton type; they were big estate cars with golden dogs penned in the back. Quite a few of the cars were driven by women. They were the kind of women who fit the description 'ladylike', and who, I imagined, drank tea from fine crockery with their little fingers cocked in the air. It was with some relief that a few minutes after driving through this wonderland, Joe spoke in his rich, sarcastic voice.

'Look like the bredren don'. reach these parts yet.'

That was all it took for the good humour between him and his spar, Bageye, to return.

'You never know, you know,' said Bageye. 'One or two might pass.'

'How you gwan know?'

172

'How you gwan know! Unless you check the cuticle.'

'For true.'

'Or put a plate-a watermelon in front of them.'

'Yeah, man. Even if it a black man a-pass for white them must take a piece.'

'Nah must.'

'But anyway, real black man couldn't live on here so.'

'How you mean?'

'Where is the Kentucky Fried Chicken, my friend?'

'Me nah see no Ladbrokes neither.'

'Tell you one t'ing though, super. Anyhow the car brock down here . . . Lawd Almighty.'

We knew that black people wouldn't be found in these parts, but Bageye told us to keep our eyes peeled nonetheless, just in case we did break down. It wasn't said as a joke.

Out on the other side of Harpenden, we passed an immaculate golf course, and just a few miles later began a slow climb up a very long, steep and windy road. The car didn't like the climb. We were all willing it not to stall. Somehow it managed to keep chugging along but at not much quicker than walking speed. It seemed impossible after several minutes that we were still ascending but we were. Any higher and I envisioned us emerging onto a plain beyond the clouds.

St Albans was the same thing again as Harpenden but bigger and a bit prissier. Even the names of the roads – King Harry's Lane, St Stephen's Hill – carried a kind of unfamiliar grandeur.

There was no more banter between our father and

Joe. Even though we were now on the level, Bageye drove very slowly. I had the feeling that any minute he might turn the car around and go back. He pulled over. Peering over his shoulder we could see why. The level was actually the crest of a hill. We were about to descend and go up another even steeper hill. It was as if we were entering the scariest part of an enormous, terrifying fairground ride.

'You t'ink we can make it?' Bageye asked.

'Well, I don't know, boss,' Joe laughed. 'Just make sure you put your foot down when we reach the bottom, and power up.'

Bageye waited till the coast was clear, until there were no cars immediately in front. As soon as we started the descent, he pushed down hard on the accelerator. I clung to Milton's arm. Milton gripped the back of the driver's seat. The car shot down and up the other side of the hill before any of us had time to be truly afraid. One more turn and we were at the entrance to the school grounds.

Another car followed on our tail so that Bageye had no alternative but to drive onto the premises of St Columba's College. Half a dozen vehicles inched forward ahead of us, arriving to pick up boys after school. The sight of them caused Joe to exclaim: 'Watch car!' His slow, reflective whistle of admiration was the same one he usually let loose when passing a pretty girl, or any girl really. He called out their names: Land Rover, Jaguar and so on. Each car snaked along the oval-shaped track which surrounded a neat, well-kept lawn. They resembled the procession of prized racehorses we sometimes witnessed on the TV parading before the race. One by one each car peeled off and slotted into the very next available parking space abutting the lawn. Bageye missed his first opportunity and then the next one. After the third, it was apparent that he was determined not to stop. We exited from the grounds but just as we rounded the corner Bageye's foot must have slipped because the car stalled, and wouldn't start again. We had no alternative but to get out and push the Mini onto the verge.

'So, what is the plan?' Joe asked.

'You tell me,' answered Bageye drily.

'Me? Is me you ask?'

Bageye wondered whether Joe could see anybody else other than the two of them.

'The plan?' said Joe. 'The five Ps, my friend: prior plan prevent poor performance. The five Ps. The plan is to listen to me when me say: "Don't buy no car from no Englishman!"'

'You nah have nothing more to say?' Bageye opened the driver's door and slammed it again with such force that the whole car rocked. He looked a little sheepishly in our direction. Joe swallowed a smile. Bageye made a point of ignoring him. 'That tie not straight,' he barked at me and set off back towards the school. Milton and I trotted behind.

'Leave me the keys,' shouted Joe. 'You never can tell.'

After so long in the car it was perhaps inevitable that Milton and I tried to trip each other up as we traipsed behind our father. We'd hardly started but Bageye had already had enough. His eyes burned hot with disappointment.

'You see you. You see you! You never understand you is being watched? Yes, bwoy, Englishman a–watch see which way you turn. You carry on like a pair of grinning monkey. The suit don't fool the Englishman. He know you is just a monkey in a suit, cyann' even walk with your head straight. Englishman say to himself: "Well, what can you expect? Just yesterday them was a–swing through tree."'

He was addressing both his sons but I was fixated on the fact that I was not wearing my suit: he could not have me in mind. Bageye was just warming up. We passed one expensive car after another and he became increasingly animated.

'See it there? When you turn big man is so you must drive. Turn big man and me ever catch you in a little kiss–me–arse car that cyann' start then is finish, I finish with you, you understand.'

Each step we took now, he would have us understand, was a step towards our destiny, not just towards St Columba's College. At the end of the driveway the glass entrance to the school bulged out like a giant fishbowl. A big-bellied priest in a black robe stood beside the doors, beaming. He gave the impression that he'd been waiting all the time just to greet us. Though the bronze crucifix adorning his chest looked serious, he wore his cassock casually, as if it was his work clothes, his overalls perhaps. He shook Bageye's hand and then Milton's and mine in that way some people did when they wanted to give the impression of something else, something more meaningful.

Brother Arnold announced himself as the headmaster: 'Here for the test?' His American accent was smooth and warm like the brandy it was easy to imagine him finishing the day with. The dozens of tiny veins that zigzagged just beneath the pale surface of his cheeks suggested a man who liked to drink. Bageye brightened when the priest addressed him as 'sir'. There was no sting in the greeting. We'd never met any Americans but both our parents held them in high regard. Unlike the Englishman, the American, they believed, was a straight shooter. When he said 'sir', he meant it. By contrast, there was something not quite right when the Englishman attempted to be respectful. It didn't come naturally to him. When he did so, he was either obsequious or excessively polite to the point of rudeness.

The headmaster caught us staring through the glass doors to the glass wall at the back of the atrium and the sight of the city centre in the distance.

'Quite a view, isn't it,' said Brother Arnold, pointing out Verulamium, the old Roman fort at the base of the school's playing fields, and then – rising up on the far side, level with the college – the medieval abbey.

'Yes, it is quite a view,' responded Bageye. I was surprised by how speaky-spokey he sounded.

We stood for a while – longer than necessary – before the headmaster leant towards me and Milton and said: 'I expect you'd like to begin.' He ushered us up the stairs, stopping in the hall to describe something of the history of the school to Bageye. Several panoramic black-and-white group photos of the school's pupil population from its first years to the present were mounted on the wall behind him, but the priest made no reference to them, and every time I craned my neck for a better look he seemed to shuffle along just enough to obscure my view. I had the queer feeling that he was trying to shield us from the photos. When we finally moved off towards the headmaster's office I stole a glance. Scanning the tiers of serious-looking boys in blazers I could not see even one dark face among them.

We were to sit the test in Brother Arnold's office. It was spartan, with plain wood-panelled walls and black and brown furniture. Venetian blinds were tilted so that little light came through. The interior would have been darker still if it hadn't been for the pane of glass cut into the thick door to the office. Milton and I were given chairs at either end of an enormous desk; and several sheets of paper and a pencil each were set in front of us. Brother Arnold wondered whether we needed anything before the test. Bageye assured him that we didn't. Did Milton want to remove his jacket?

'No,' answered Bageye. It was also 'no' to the question of whether Bageye wanted to wish his sons luck? His sons didn't need luck, he said, because 'prior plan prevent poor performance'. The priest escorted our father outside and, closing the door, let us know that we had exactly an hour to complete the exam.

Though it was nearing dusk it was light enough to read the questions, but the dimness of the office was oppressive. I wanted very much to switch on the ceiling light but could not move from the chair. I whispered to Milton that, as he was the elder child, he should get up and turn it on but he too was unsure of whether it was allowed. I pleaded with him but he had stopped listening and was busy scribbling on the first sheet.

I straightened my papers and sharpened and resharpened the pencil. There were no photos on the desk or vases for flowers, and no certificates on the walls, just a clock whose hands appeared not to move. Occasionally muffled chattering could be heard outside the door and a couple of times half-familiar eyes flitted across the saucer-sized glass panel in the door. I reordered the papers and sharpened the pencil once more. The next time I looked at the clock, bizarrely, it was an hour later. I could hear the sound of Brother Arnold's heels clacking along the corridor and steadily approaching, and though I hadn't noticed him leaving his seat I caught sight of Milton out of the corner of my eye scurrying back towards the chair. Brother Arnold entered and immediately flicked the switch turning on the ceiling light. I thought I would be sick, actually sick. It did not happen, nor the sudden unexpected heart attack that I hoped somehow to bring on, nor the spontaneous collapse onto the floor that would break a limb. There were no sirens and no ambulance. Brother Arnold held out his hand for the papers. I was sure that I had hardly written anything yet there were words and numbers scrawled all over the papers. I did not recognise the handwriting.

The headmaster quickly looked through the test papers, and just minutes later he opened the door and summoned Bageye who had been waiting outside. It must have been him who'd earlier peered through the window in the door, and I was perplexed that I somehow hadn't realised. Milton and I stood and gave up our seats to Brother Arnold and Bageye. Before sitting down the headmaster went over and extended a hand to Bageye: 'Congratulations, you have two bright boys.' Bageye looked stunned, like a poker player whose bluff had been called by a better hand.

'Now let me ask you,' said Brother Arnold, 'why do you want to send your boys to this school?'

Bageye stared directly ahead. He struggled even to form his lips into shape for the beginning of a response. He looked hard at Brother Arnold as if searching for the answer on his face. It was not beyond possibility that Bageye actually objected to the question and had no intention of answering. When he did speak, it was almost as a whisper.

'Well, you know, me never even pass worms,' said Bageye. 'Me want a different life for my boys. Want them to have the opportunity that me never have.' Our father spoke on and on in this vein, freely in a way that we had never witnessed him speak with a white person before, or any person, for that matter.

'I had an office job!' Bageye said, and he laughed at the memory of it now. 'When I was seventeen I went to the manager and said I wanted to go to sea. And he said: "What, you want to be a dutty seaman?" But I had made my mind up. Well, after six months at sea I decided I didn't like it so I wrote to the manager for my old job back, and he said: "No, you must stick and stay." When me start I was a galley boy and by the time me leave I was a second steward, had maybe half a dozen men under me. Even gave orders to white men. Them never like it but them have to obey. That's it. Second steward, and now on the production line at Vauxhall Motors. Well, sir, my boy them not gwan work in no factory and them not gwan drive a second-hand car that conk out every five minute.'

180

Bageye said no more. His final words drifted round the room and seemed to settle on our shoulders and chests. Eventually Brother Arnold hauled himself out of his chair like a man emerging from a deep sleep, and passed a school prospectus to our father.

'As you'll have two sons in the school, the first will require a full fee but the second is required only to meet two-thirds of the full amount.'

'That's all right.'

'No, I don't think you understand,' said the headmaster. 'This is a standard arrangement.'

Bageye stood up and shook the priest's hand firmly. 'It's all right,' he repeated. 'We can manage.'

Brother Arnold tried to interrupt but Bageye wouldn't let him. We made our exit with a further round of handshakes. When we got back to the car, we found Joe sitting in the driver's seat. The engine was purring, and looking between the two men it was difficult to tell who was beaming more – Joe or Bageye.

Mismatch

'IF YOU CYANN' LEARN, THEN you will feel.'
   Bageye couldn't have put it more plainly. The
warning had long been on record. Unlearnt lessons
of unacceptable behaviour, that is repeat offences,
would not be tolerated and would result in punishment.
Simple so. But the difficulty was that there was no
accord reached among us children about how far you
could go before transgressing. Take the argument, for
instance, about what volume on the TV would
penetrate the ceiling and floor above and ultimately
seep into Bageye's sleeping soul. The confidence of
the boldest and most defiant who fiddled dangerously
with the dial like a safe-cracker, turning up the volume,
evaporated on the first sound of a piece of furniture
scraping across the floor upstairs. Immediately then,
someone would spring up and readjust the volume
downwards. There was no time to do anything else.
But by then it was too late.

   There were sixteen steps on the staircase from the
landing to the hallway. As our father descended, the
groan of each step was more terrible than the last.
Until he appeared at the door of the dining room
where we co-conspirators were huddled in front of
the silent TV. 'You see, onoo. I done tell you already,'
Bageye cursed. A film of eye-water (the remains of
sleep) that had collected in the cusp of his lids oscillated

as he spoke. Anyone brave enough to look would have seen signs of smouldering; that this afternoon, oil had been added to the mix of eye-water and a torch set to it. His eyes were aflame.

'You see, onoo. If you cyann' learn, then you will feel.'

Bageye looked over to me and Milton. Since the entrance exam he had seemed ever more alert to us, and to conduct unbecoming to the young gentlemen that we were now destined to be. He walked over to the TV. He took his time but it was obvious what was coming. He reached behind the television set; unplugged it from the socket; wrapped the end of the lead around one hand and used the other hand, with one swift yank, to wrench the plug off the lead. He discarded the severed lead, thrust the plug into his cardigan pocket and made his way back towards his bedroom.

That was at 3.30 p.m. About an hour later there was a knock at the front door which we didn't recognise. When it was apparent that no one was going to answer, Selma puffed out her cheeks like an angry fish, put on her adult, irritated voice and drawled wearily: 'Somebody at the door.' More and more Selma was 'coming like the Queen bee': she had spoken. It didn't matter that Mum had gone to the shops, leaving her in charge in case the house 'burn down'; Selma was in that mood now where whosoever was knocking could bang until the door came off its hinges for all she cared, she wasn't going to budge. Besides, she was nicely positioned in front of the electric fire, and flouting the rules, had flicked down the switch, so that both bars were blazing, for maximum heat.

Milton stared blankly at the TV even though it was off. It was as if he was in a trance; in so deep that the sound waves travelling from the front door did not register. You had to admit, it was pretty impressive.

Actually we were all down deep, following the earlier unscheduled visit from our father, with hardly a sound except the constant whispered instructions to 'Shhh!'. It was funny, this 'Shhh' business. You heard it over and over again. And after a while, when you listened back, you thought, that's funny, it sounds like my voice, sounds like me. It was kind of routine. Often I imagined that downstairs in the dining room, with all the 'Shhhing' and with the TV turned down so low that it might just as well have been muted, we were like the crew of a U-boat creeping along close to the bottom of the ocean; upstairs, the naval destroyer, HMS *Bageye*, was ready to drop depth charges or fire off torpedoes at the first sound of a disturbance.

The front door rattled again, and we all strained our ears for the awful suggestion of any stirring up above. The moment was fast approaching where further resistance would be impossible to sustain: the danger was too great. Selma glowered at me until my resolve broke, as she knew it would. The settee gave me up, and I moved all too quickly from stubborn refusal to the queasily familiar total surrender.

'About time!' said Selma.

I stamped out to the kitchen. Something snapped in Milton. The centripetal force of the TV box suddenly released him and tenderly, he called me back. Yes, I thought, his conscience was killing him. Of course! He was going to volunteer in my place. There was a God. I returned wide-eyed and grateful. Milton looked at me with genuine pity but then simply whispered: 'Look first!'

On the other side of the front door, through the curtained-off, oblong insert of frosted glass, Billy Brooks, the boxing coach, should have been easy to make out from his bulk.

My father claimed he often had difficulty telling the difference between all the white people he had the misfortune to run across, pointing out that 'all-a dem look grey'. But as this six-foot, fifteen-stone former boxer, and now builder, stood on the concrete step, bouncing up and down on the balls of his toes, strengthening his calves, the chances of my convincing Bageye that Brooksy was actually the scoutmaster or the priest seemed slim. For as Bageye was fond of repeating to any child mad enough to play fast with the truth: 'You think I born yesterday; it forty-eight years ago I born!'

Since the trip to St Albans, Bageye had drawn up a new set of rules. Out of school hours, sporting activity, boxing in particular, had been outlawed at 42 Castlecroft Road. We were not to misunderstand our father. Along with all the other fellas, he threw his arms in the air and cheered when Muhammad Ali pounded poor old Henry Cooper beyond the point where he could still be recognised. Ali, after all, was 'one of we'. The Louisville Lip was born at a time of few opportunities for the black man. 'But this is a new era, my friend,' said Bageye. Our father wasn't planning on private education for his pickney only for them 'to end up just as the man expec'', only able to employ their fists. No man, Bageye didn't leave his warm bed each night, step out into the cold and trudge his unwilling body onto the floor of the production line on the night shift just so us pickney could 'let the white man tek you mek fool, bash out your brain in the boxing ring, pat you on the head and throw you a banana while him pocket the lion share of the purse'. Uh-huh, if the man wanted a jackass to ride he must look elsewhere.

The Boy Scouts was still permitted but the football and boxing clubs were now off limits. Neither I nor my brother could now remember whose brilliant idea it was to defy our father and secretly continue with the boxing club. Nothing was said but lately the tension between us had grown out of the nervousness that one of us was bound to slip up and give the game away; or more likely arrive inevitably at the idea that it was wiser to be the first to volunteer the information of the offence, to turn Queen's evidence, as it were, against your accomplice, in the hope that it might lessen the punishment which was surely heading your way. There was no code of silence, no Mafia *omertà*. Subject to the slightest bit of pressure, each of us siblings was likely to squeal.

Secretly, we were both working out what we might say. But if I was a betting man I'd have put everything on Milton triumphing. I hadn't yet perfected my storytelling. Recent examples made me wince when I thought back on them. For example, there was the letter I was supposed to have posted but which had gone missing because, I claimed, some vandal had pushed a flaming match into the slit of the postbox just after, setting all the letters ablaze.

Bageye was snoring upstairs in the small room at the back of the house. There was another knock at the front door. It was a respectful knock, perhaps even a little timid, as if the caller doubted he was at the correct address. Milton followed me towards the door but at the sound of the boxing instructor calling out, he held back. Suddenly, he doubled up as though he was suffering from an attack of stomach cramp or an urgent need to pee.

In between the rasps of his breath I could hear him thinking, making plans. The knocking continued. It had to be stopped. I stepped out to face Billy Brooks and pulled the door behind me until it was virtually closed. Not fully, because then I wouldn't have been able to hear the squeak of the stairs which would mean my brother had reverted to playing Tonto to my Lone Ranger. I often considered us partnered like the inseparable noble cowboy and his trusty Indian. We both claimed to be the Lone Ranger but Tonto was a closer fit. At such times of crisis we called to mind the old joke: Tonto and the Lone Ranger ride into a deserted canyon. It's a trap! The Lone Ranger turns to his compadre and cries: 'Quick, Tonto, we're surrounded by Indians.' And Tonto says coolly: 'What do you mean we, white man?'

Any squeak would suggest brother Tonto was mounting the stairs to alert Chief Bageye, to confess and concede his minor role and guilt in the massive disgrace unfolding on the doorstep, of which I was the major author.

Billy Brooks wanted to come in and see my parents. I started to speak. I started but failed to finish the sentence. Eventually, I jumbled some words together which made no sense. And then silence. The lull was broken by the grating sound of the bolt of the back gate being slid open, and somebody entering the narrow corridor – which separated our terraced house from the neighbours, and into which no light ever penetrated. Suddenly Tonto shot out from its dark interior. He flashed past Brooksy and me without looking in our direction and zipped round the corner into the Robinsons' at number 44.

Brooksy was obviously puzzled. I could tell because he did that adult gesture of tilting his head back slightly, thrusting out his arms and turning his hands palm up.

'Wasn't that Milton?' When I didn't answer, he continued: 'Well, actually it was you I wanted to speak to anyway.' I looked beyond him to his car which was parked twenty yards away close to the rec.

Billy Brooks always gave the impression of being amused, as if he was enjoying some quiet, private joke. Like Knight, he'd been a semi-professional boxer but there were no marks on his face: it was smooth, almost translucent; and his eyebrows and lashes were so fair they seemed to disappear. In some regards, though he wore no collar, Billy Brooks could have been a priest. Not only did he have the kind of soothing voice that invited confession, but he was graced with soft hands and clean fingernails. There was a delicacy about him which belied the rumours every kid in the boxing club repeated about his youthful, earlier life as a bone-crushing bruiser in the ring.

Brooksy climbed into the driver's seat, and turned the ignition. I hesitated, and he leant over and pushed ajar the passenger-side door. When I still didn't move, he cut the engine. 'We don't have to go anywhere,' he said. 'We can just sit and talk.' I glanced back towards the house. If anyone was peeking through the curtains then they couldn't be seen. I took a chance and jumped into the passenger seat, then slid down onto the floor. Brooksy swallowed a laugh. Only when he had composed himself sufficiently did he begin to speak, addressing the top of my head.

'I'll not be joining you down there.' After another few minutes of silence he tried again.

'So, what was it you wanted to talk about?' he teased.

He shook his head as he continued now in a strangely probing but faraway voice: 'Hard lines . . . about the other night. Hard lines.'

It was one of his most repeated phrases. 'Hard lines' was Scottish for 'bad luck'. He said it almost as a reflex, whenever a boy was beaten in the ring. Dazed and disappointed, the defeated boxer probably couldn't take it in. But even though I was determined to focus exclusively on the dashboard in front of my nose, I could tell that Brooksy really meant it. He was the most tender man I ever met.

'Mixie Dunn had to go to the hospital,' said Brooksy. 'I hear his earlobe was hanging off.' It almost sounded as if Brooksy approved.

'Sorry about that,' I answered. 'Did they manage to sew it back on?'

'Aye.' Billy Brooks rested a soft hand on the back of my head. 'But I doubt he'll be troubling you again.'

I pulled myself up into the passenger seat. In defiance of the promise to myself, I could hear the truth gathering at the back of my throat, and it wasn't long before it began to work its way out: words detailing the horrible chanting that had started things off, the fight, the whole embarrassing story.

The chanting began on the way back from the boxing club's day trip to Clacton-on-Sea. Brooksy had hired a forty-seat coach, and together with some friends – brought along as marshals – he'd managed to keep us not only amused but also in check, relatively; in between the fairground rides, we were herded together and prevented from any rampage through the seaside resort. Perhaps with the strain of this alien, Herculean effort of self-control, it was inevitable that something broke in some of the wilder crowd on the return journey. Boys sitting at the back of the bus started making monkey noises which – my brother and I only realised gradually and with increments of embarrassment – were aimed in our direction, and which the mimics evidently thought hilarious. Though I doubt whether they understood the subtleties of the insult. 'Monkey' was what some light-skinned black people called the real coal-black brethren. You hoped to escape the classification in the next generation but no one was fooled. As Mum would say: 'Every monkey t'ink him pickney white.'

That Mixie Dunn, who was not known for his sophistication, was the chief instigator of the chants came as no surprise. Mixie was the hardest of the hard nuts. He had a reputation for invincibility. But he hadn't been held by his ankles like Achilles and lowered into immortalising waters; he'd been dipped in bile. Mixie was so called because he liked to 'mix it'; he may have been only so-so in the ring but in the streets he was the very last boy you'd want to mix it with; it was rumoured that he'd even mixed it with boys a couple of years older. He'd probably have mixed it with anybody – even an adult.

Mixie Dunn needed little provocation. He had an uncanny ability to know when you were staring at him; it was a gift unique to him and certainly a mystery to the eyeballer who was likely to be gobbed at or kicked in the shins or both. The trouble was you couldn't help yourself because the sour-faced Mixie drew your attention, mostly by his disgusting personal habits. Picking a scab before it'd completely crusted over, breaking off a piece and chewing it, was his favourite pastime. True, he wasn't sophisticated but in some ways he was more adult than most; it wouldn't have occurred to any other boy that there was sport to be had from making monkey noises at the Grants. He had a talent for it. In the last half-hour of the journey, Mixie rolled out a whole repertoire of chants that ranged from chimpanzee to baboon. Soon a chorus had started up with some others. Perhaps not unexpectedly, the chants also came from the formerly loyal lips of David Synott.

Some boys you liked for their fathers. 'As we're going to be in the same class,' David Synott had announced when we first met, 'we might as well be friends.' But if it hadn't been for Mr Synott I'd have kept my distance from his crafty son. David was the kind of boy who made a point of bringing along a huge bottle of lemonade on a summer's-day school outing, and when the sun was high and your own provisions long gone, he'd taunt you with the near-full bottle; when you begged him for a swig he'd charge you tuppence for a sip, just a sip, mind.

I made allowance for David because his father was such a prince. He wasn't much taller than us. And whereas David was podgy and moon-faced, his pa was a wiry man: there was more fat on a chip, as they say, than on him. What immediately struck you about Mr Synott was that he seemed to have reached his ultimate age; he'd a face like cracked leather, and was probably no more than fifty, but he was never going to get any older, or appear to get any older, a bit like Bageye really.

Old Man Synott didn't really belong in a town; there was something of the Irish bog about him still. He reeked of cigarettes and damp soil; as if he'd put on clothes washed in tobacco after taking a mud bath. An invisible layer of Kerry earth clung to him. He'd shake his head mystified, absolutely mystified by the perfect hedges and flower-beds of chrysanthemums that adorned the neighbours' lovingly mowed front lawns. For his part, much to David's embarrassment, Mr Synott had turned his patch of land over to something that looked more like an allotment.

Despite talk of some tragedy about his mother, it was almost impossible to feel sorry for David Synott because he was always using his brains on you. When he wanted you to do something for him, somehow you always found yourself dropping everything; but if you needed something from him, well, he wouldn't even fart on you. The afternoon before Clacton-on-Sea, David cornered me after school. He'd come across a stack of turf that had been abandoned. He had a plan. He pleaded with me to help him cart back some of the turf and roll it out over his yard. An hour later, after much grunting and stamping into place, the result wasn't quite the Wimbledon-like carpet of grass we'd imagined but a lumpy lunar-landscape mess.

Nonetheless, David and I stood proudly to attention as Old Man Synott came round the corner, home from work. We were expecting points, at least, for effort; but his father was full of rage and tears, though not about the imperfect patchwork quilt of turf rather his thoughts were turned towards the poor suffocating vegetables crushed beneath the newly laid lawn. I escaped with a dark look but he gave his son an earful, and then some. Eventually, like a child who cries himself to sleep, Mr Synott gave up complaining. He went inside and quickly downed a bottle of stout. It was probably more than one bottle because it was half an hour before we saw him again. He came back out from the gate at the side of the house pushing a wheelbarrow. He parked up and took a pair of shovels from the barrow and handed one to each of us. 'Ah well, I don't suppose it'll be as long to take up as it was to put down.' He held onto my shovel. 'You'll be staying for dinner.' It was said more as a command than a request.

He stood guard over us, quenching his thirst with an unending supply of bottles of stout, magically freed from trouser pockets. In between bottles he belched good-naturedly, while we slowly and unenthusiastically began (without gloves) to pull up the oblong patches of turf (glistening with squiggy worms) and restore them to their original, giant Swiss-roll shape.

There was one other thing on his mind that Mr

Synott wondered whether I could help him with. It was about the boxing tournament due to take place the following weekend.

'Say I was to come to you, and say I know a fella thinking of a small bet on one of the bouts. I'm just philosophising now, mind. Suppose this fella was to come to me and say, "I'm thinking of putting five pounds on young Grant." What do you suppose I should say to the fella?'

I had never lost a boxing match, and couldn't foresee a time when I ever would.

'I'm just philosophising, you understand. But what would you say?'

'Double it,' I answered.

'Say that again,' said Mr Synott excitedly. 'What you just said. Say that again.'

'Double it.'

'Double it?' Mr Synott mouthed to himself. He made a triumphant fist, pushed out an index finger and jabbed it into his son's shoulder. 'You hear that, David? Double it. The quality of the man. The quality of the man.'

Immediately we were done with the turf, Mr Synott took out a trowel from the barrow. He held it up, considered both of us, and smartly handed the trowel to his son (winking at me as he did so) and bid him make a start on digging up the carrots, onions and potatoes. David shot me a fierce, hot and hurt look. After what seemed an interminable time stabbing at the earth, he passed the first liberated onion to his father. The old man broke the cake of dirt from it and for a brief moment stood admiring it the way we all did when a loaf first came out of the oven.

'What do you fellas say to a cheese and onion sandwich?'

Though Mr Synott's sense of hospitality was highly developed, the details weren't always adhered to: he had a nasty habit of missing out some vital ingredient when it came to rustling up the tea. The sandwiches, when they came, proved hard to chew without the apparently optional extra cheese, and both of us spent an equal amount of time scraping away the bits of bread that stuck to the roofs of our mouths.

We were saved from a second round of onion sandwiches by the arrival of Mr Fitzsimons. He'd been to the house – David later told me – almost every day that week to admire and play on the snooker table (set up in the dining room) that he and Mr Synott had bought in partnership together the week before. But Fitz wasn't his usual jaunty self. His wife, it seemed, had just found out about the table and there was trouble at home. Nothing that a game of snooker shouldn't be able to shift, his business partner ventured. After all, snooker put everything into perspective. Fitz had got everything upside down, arse-ways backwards. Mr Synott took out his first ciggy for the evening to better ponder the conundrum. There were degrees of awkwardness, he argued: a little difficulty with the missus paled beside a maximum snooker break. Once Fitz slammed a few snooker balls into pockets and headed towards an uninterrupted, unassailable break, then anything would seem possible. Mr Fitzsimons was not convinced. His wife had told him to get rid of the table and to insist on his money back. David and I sat in the living room as they continued to argue.

'We have to sell.'

'Don't be daft, man,' said Mr Synott. 'It can't be done.'

'Well, half of it's mine,' pleaded Fitz.

'Half of it's yours, you say?'

'Yes, yes, I want my half share.'

'Half of it's yours?'

'Yes!'

Back and forth they went until Mr Synott suddenly threw down his snooker cue onto the table. He went out the back to his garden shed and returned moments later with an axe.

'Where were we?' said Mr Synott coldly.

'I'm sorry,' Fitz shook his head, 'but I have to get back half of what's mine.'

'You want your share?'

'Yes!' Fitz screamed. 'I want my half.'

'You want your half?'

'Yes!'

Mr Synott lifted up the axe and in one swift movement brought it crashing down clean through the middle of the snooker table. 'Which half do you want?'

The following evening, with the monkey chants ringing in my ears, I thought of the purity of Mr Synott's gesture with the axe as my foot collided with his son's posterior. David had just stepped down from the bus when I landed the first kick. In a long straggly line all of us boys from the club proceeded towards home. I continued to lift my foot to David's backside at regular intervals along the way. It served as punctuation to my monologue about how remarkable it was that monkeys were able to kick. After about a hundred yards David spoke, only half turning back towards me in between the jolts. 'It wasn't just me. Mixie started it. Why don't you pick on Mixie?'

It was not an unreasonable point – though, of course, to act on David's suggestion carried the obvious danger of finding myself on the receiving end of violence rather than unilaterally dispensing it.

Mixie Dunn was a little further up ahead. I picked up my pace, hurrying towards him before I could change my mind. When close enough, I shoved him on the shoulder. Mixie wheeled sharply, as if he'd half been expecting some sort of challenge but was still surprised. 'What! You want some?'

The concrete pavement looked dangerous and forbidding. What would happen if my head crashed on the ground? 'Not here,' I said, pointing to a triangle of soft grass at the corner of the next street. 'Over there.'

The rest of the boys fanned out, as if on a secret signal, and formed an impromptu ring of spectators. Though everyone understood (and Brooksy had wanted to spell out to my parents) that I was something of a prodigy and by far the best boxer in the club, Mixie seemed much more formidable than usual; he also appeared more irritated than angry. He stood hands on hips, looking on. It dawned on me now that I had never had a fight outside the ring. Its inevitability brought on a kind of relief. But what was suddenly unnerving – now that the fight was settled – was the looming possibility that in ten or twenty minutes, or however long it took, I'd be returning home with in all likelihood torn and bloodied clothing; yet I was unsure of my father's whereabouts. If he was already at home, then the jig was up. The boxing club had been outlawed; never mind fighting in the street.

In my father's unwritten style-book, creating a public spectacle was to be avoided at all costs. Bageye was never amused by drunks, the way the English were. Seeing through the good-humoured bluff of the 'last-orders' revellers stopping off at the off-licence to see them through the journey home, he'd lament: 'Only ignorant fellas carry on so.' Exposure to the coarseness of the culture was one of the hazards of living on Farley Hill, he'd explain, but we mustn't confuse living there with being from there. Our condition on Farley Hill was temporary, after all; and brushing away Mum's cynicism, he'd address us children directly: 'Don't get too comfortable, you hear. We're only passing through.'

Imagine then one of Bageye's pickney street-fighting? You joke! Better that someone came and whispered to him that they'd caught you smoking at a bus stop or emptying your nose, like the Cha-cha man, on the side of the road. The very idea would have been enough to sicken Bageye's stomach. Even then my father would have given the informant one look, a gorgonising look, and run him because such a thing was beyond the possible. But, as I squared up to Mixie Dunn, I couldn't back out now: the trap was of my own making.

One or two friends were dotted around the spectators, but the rest appeared a circle of hostile natives, and into the middle stepped the fiercest and most cruel brave, Mixie. I spied Milton peeling away from the group; after a few yards he started to run. I hoped he was heading back to the bus to get a grown-up's help. In the meantime, there was no option except to begin.

I adopted the boxing stance: left foot forward; right fist under my chin and left fist held out, ready to jab in accordance with Queensberry rules. Suddenly Mixie ran up and leapt feet first towards me, catching my shins and bringing me down.

Anyone passing would have been surprised by the strange howling that seemed to be coming from me – a prolonged and pitiful sound of shock. Mixie's confusing, unsportsmanlike assault allowed for none of the skills of the ring; there could be no aesthetically pleasing jab or graceful avoidance of an opponent's clumsy lunge. I suppose it was closer to wrestling; pulling, ripping, butting with elbows, knees and lastly the head, so that after thirty seconds – no more – there was the first intimation of blood streaming from my nose.

It is a queer sensation to be subject to a pummelling with the realisation that the outcome, the severity of the pain and its duration, is beyond your control. At least inside the ring the trauma is circumscribed: there are only three rounds, each lasting a couple of minutes, and if things get really bad the referee will show mercy and step in. What's more, a ring is bound by rope, but we thrashed about on the grass, edging perilously close to the pavement. I feared those concrete slabs as the dreamer does a precipice.

And then a miracle. Mixie was pulled up and lifted from me as if by a crane. The arms of the crane belonged to Mrs Dunn. Milton appeared grinning beside her. No doubt I'd be reminded for weeks on end about his role in the rescue. But the truth was that Mrs Dunn had been wandering home with some friends from the social club when she spotted the melee, and had leapt in unaware that her son was involved. I'd always liked Mrs Dunn. There was something plain, simple and honest about her, just like her smell: boiled cabbage and potatoes. Increasingly, I came to see that folks like Mrs Dunn and Mr Synott presented a perfect conundrum: you could never look at the parent and account for the son.

I scrambled to my feet and one of the boys put my arm round his neck and shoulder. We'd gone some distance before I realised that my prop, my Simon of Cyrene, was none other than David Synott. 'Didn't know you could fight like that,' he said admiringly. 'Mixie came off the worse.'

Back at David's house, we passed the living room. Mr Synott was sleeping heavily, splayed out on the sofa like a Hollywood gangster blasted by a shotgun. His son steered me towards the kitchen where he fetched a wash rag. He ran it under the tap and started ever so gently to clean away some of the blood on my forehead. I recoiled at the whiteness of the flannel. It would be ruined but David insisted.

On the way back, Milton walked sulkily in front of me. We had yet to reach agreement on a strategy for re-entering the house undetected. He was playing it close to the wire but slowed now, just enough, so that I might catch up before we arrived at Castlecroft Road.

'Round the back. And you go first.'

There was no time to argue with him. We crept down the alleyway and climbed over the back gate. The back door was locked, so I hauled myself up the drainpipe and squeezed head first through a narrow kitchen window, thankfully left open at the top. It was quite a drop to the sink and the rest of my body followed, plopping down like the tail of a snake with an unfortunate thud.

I unlocked the back door. Milton slipped in and we slid along the hallway to the stairs. With safety almost in sight, my brother edged in front of me. I wasn't too worried because we were both skilled in the art of silently ascending the staircase. His foot hovered over the first step but on contact, it made a sharp squeak. My father immediately called out my name.

Bageye was in the living room, on the settee, holding and reading intently one of the volumes of the big blue illustrated encyclopaedia, the ones with the embossed covers and the crest of some aristocratic family or university stamped on the first page. In all our years together, I never saw him read another book. Apart from the racing supplement of the newspaper, the encyclopaedia was the only thing he ever read. He studied solemnly the racing pages with a tiny blue pen used to mark up a fancied horse or jockey but he took pleasure in reading the encyclopaedia, especially when it offered a chance to suggest a correction. 'A ruler is something like a king or queen,' my father would say, snatching from a child the twelve-inch piece of wood or plastic which we annoyingly kept on misnaming. He'd hold it up and announce: 'This is a rule.'

My sweaty hand had trouble turning the handle on the living-room door. The lock kept slipping back, so that my entrance was much more laboured than hoped for. Despite this, my father did not look up as the door clicked back behind me. It was not a good sign. Bageye balanced the encyclopaedia on its spine and let it fall so that it appeared to open at a random page. Church people did something like this when they threw down the Bible and it landed on a passage of scripture that seemed miraculously to have been predetermined, to have been personally selected for them, hallelujah. Except in this case, when you looked more closely, the encyclopaedia had opened worryingly at the same page as the red ribbon marker.

'You 'ave anyt'ing you want to tell me?' he asked.

Even though the hundreds of pages inside were extremely thin – almost transparent – just like cigarette paper, the encyclopaedia was thick. Bageye lifted the page with delicate fingers. I can honestly say I was as shocked as he must have been when he first saw it. In the top right-hand corner a two-inch square piece was missing.

'Wha' happen, you t'ink?' my father wanted to know. He pushed the encyclopaedia across the glass table towards me.

I would have liked to have suggested that 'the Devil is a bad man', which was what our mother often said when things went inexplicably wrong and there was no obvious culprit in sight. But it was dawning on me that I should forget the bruising that was beginning to take shape more solidly on my forehead and under my right cheek; that this business with the encyclopaedia was far more serious.

My father was a man of long patience but he didn't like to ask a question twice. I focused on the page. Lately, I'd been working on my expressions, and now could passably set my face somewhere between respectful curiosity and mild disinterest.

'It looks like somebody's taken a pair of scissors,' I said in my most matter-of-fact voice, 'and cut out the drawing of the butterfly from the page.' But even for 42 Castlecroft Road it was a peculiar act. A blasé attitude was the very last I should have adopted. It needed to be corrected. 'Who would do such a thing?' I lamented. My father did not display any emotion and seemed to pay little attention to my make-believe incredulity. I imagined him thinking: *But wait! You t'ink I born yesterday. Is forty-eight years ago I born.*

He twisted his lips, biting the insides: 'A butterfly? How you know it a butterfly, super?' The casualness of his question took me by surprise. I could not speak, and though I was still standing, I felt somehow that I was collapsing in on myself. My thoughts raced ahead like a set of gears where numerous combinations are explored but none will mesh; or the dream where, in desperation for escape, a series of doors are tried and each opens onto a brick wall. The silence must have lasted some little while because suddenly Bageye spoke in an unfriendly voice: 'Is wha'appen, you don't have tongue in your head?' He seemed to grow more and more irritable. Instinctively, he reached for his tobacco tin and started on the slow but satisfying process of building a roll-up. But I shouldn't make the mistake of thinking we could change the subject. 'OK, hold that one for now. We wheel and come back to that,' he warned. 'What about Lepidoptera?' My father wanted to find out whether I knew the meaning of the word 'Le-pi-dop-tera'. I didn't. His eyes flashed coldly across me: 'So, remind me again, me frien'. How you know it a butterfly? Take your time. You want some water?'

It was really hard lines. Out of all the hundreds of pages in the encyclopaedia, remarkably, my father had stumbled across the entry for the 'order of insects with four membranous scale-covered wings'. And yet though ignorant of the word Lepidoptera, I'd let slip that I knew it was related to butterflies. How so?

It was difficult to explain. Well, to begin with, let's say there were times even when you knew you were doing something wrong, you still felt compelled to continue. You might say to yourself; *Well, it's just a little thing, just a pea.* But the trouble was my peas had grown in number over the months. If I was to string them together, that necklace would be dangling down by my navel. To answer my father about my knowledge of the missing butterfly, I would have had to explain that somehow it had flown miraculously from the encyclopaedia to the lined pages of my homework book.

So much time had elapsed without my being able to conjure an acceptable answer that I began to notice a dimming of the light through the bay windows. Bageye always resisted surrendering to the inevitability of dusk coming on. Though you might think of him as a creature of the night, there was a real sense that Bageye believed that the night was a betrayal of the day. The point had passed where he should have drawn the curtains and put on the light, and the dying light cast his face in an early evening gloom. Until finally I was told: 'Hit the switch, nah man.' If he saw me properly (wounds and all) for the first time, then he simply noted it, nothing more. He wasn't ready to let

204

go of the encyclopaedia business. He was getting ready to pounce or pronounce.

'Headucation is not a joke-joke thing. Nothing a-go so. Headucation, you t'ink it a joke?'

Whenever Bageye inserted an invisible 'h' before education he did so knowingly. It wasn't like all of the fellas who put an unwarranted 'h' before any word beginning with a vowel. He did so with style and for clarification. After all, knowledge and 'studyration' had to do with the head, right?

He pulled back the encyclopaedia across the table to his side. 'You see this? You know how much night shift I work for this? Overtime. Extra time. Time and a half. Double time. Work some good money. And for what?' He held the edge of the page between his index finger and thumb and let it fall on the opened palm of his other hand. He was tender with it as if examining the broken wing of a favourite bird.

'Lucky it's just one page,' I suggested.

But he shook his head forlornly. 'It spoil. You cyann' see it spoil? No man, everything mash up. Cyann' fix again.'

I had never seen my father so blue. For a brief moment, though rationally I knew it was an impossibility, I feared he would cry.

I had a theory about my father. In his mind he had drawn up a ledger of his life divided into two halves. On one side were debits and on the other credits. The credits included his spars, gambling and driving. On the deficit side were all of the people he owed money to, my mother and most of the children. That list was growing. I imagined his hand poised over the ledger when it came to the decision about where my name should be placed.

'Perhaps if we could find the butterfly,' I suggested, 'we could Sellotape it back in.'

My father examined the front and back of the page. Very, very slowly, he started to tear the page from the encyclopaedia. The ripping sound was awful. When he had freed the page, he folded it in half and proceeded to make a paper aeroplane out of it. I didn't realise that he knew how. My father had never done anything playful like that before. It was a pretty good effort, actually. When finished, he held it by the underbelly and flicked it into the air. It landed by the door. I was unsure at first but then hastily decided to go and retrieve it. Perhaps he'd throw it again. I held out the paper plane for my father to take back but he made no movement. Bageye looked me over, and then right through me. It was as if he was making up his mind whether to surrender to the inevitable and place me in the deficit column. There was nothing more to say. He waved me away, and I walked carefully backwards towards the door, just in case I had misread his gesture, releasing me from further investigation.

I mounted the stairs and climbed into bed beside my brother. Immediately, Milton started tapping me on the shoulder. At first, I resisted, declining to respond. He obviously wanted to know what had gone on downstairs. When the tapping became too much, I kept my back to him so that he would not see that I was lying when I said: 'I confessed to everything. Told him about the fight, everything.'

Milton seemed both dismayed and disappointed by the news that somehow I had avoided punishment. As far as he was concerned it confirmed his growing suspicion about my favoured status. Looking up to the ceiling, he gave a high whistle: 'Boy, you think I could ever let him know something like that? You mad! Blood would flow.'

The next morning the encyclopaedia had disappeared from the living room. Bageye never mentioned it again.

By the time I'd finished telling Billy Brooks the whole sorry tale I was completely drained. I'd never been so tired in my life. But it wasn't over yet. Peculiarly, Brooksy wanted to know how I felt about it all now.

'Strange,' I said.

'Strange?'

'I can't explain.'

'Try. Do you mean about the fight or about your father?'

You see, this was the trouble with telling anything to anybody, especially kindly white people. It was never enough. You allowed a story to leak out, one drip at a time. Before long they wanted the tap turned on full. Brooksy could stay there 'lick him chops'. After all, he would not have to answer for what was said later back inside 42 Castlecroft Road.

My mother would regularly accuse Bageye of being overly fond of gossip. 'That man like chat people business too much,' she would grumble. But Bageye didn't like other people chatting our business. We knew better than to carry news on the road about anything that went on within the four walls of Castlecroft Road. While Billy Brooks was pumping me for even more information, it occurred to me that the time was getting on; that it was close to or even past 5 o'clock – when my father would have to get up for the night shift. I was nervous and it showed. Brooksy caught me, once too often, looking over my shoulder.

'You've a bad case of the Messerschmidt twitch there,' he teased. 'No one's going to shoot you down like a Spitfire pilot. We're just talking, right. Two people, just talking?'

I didn't answer, so Brooksy continued: 'I imagine you feel you've let yourself down a bit; that it needn't have happened. Is that how you feel?'

It was weird because Billy Brooks was exactly right. But I couldn't tell him. It wasn't necessarily because he was a white man that you couldn't ultimately trust him, but he was definitely too kind. Yes, I might have said, it was just like the time I broke my collarbone. I'd never broken anything before. I knew it would heal but I'd never be whole again. That purity had gone. It'd never be the same.

'I think you're being a bit harsh on yourself, lad,' Brooksy said. I was keen to leave the car but Billy Brooks wouldn't let me go until I'd agreed to put the fight with Mixie behind me. He also made me pledge that I wasn't going to give up on the club, and that I'd still take part in the boxing match planned for the coming Saturday night. 'This is important,' he said finally, with a heavy voice. 'Promise me this. Never lose the taste of yourself.'

I got out and pushed the door closed, firm enough to shut it but carefully so that the slam wouldn't be heard inside the house. Billy Brooks started to pull away, too slowly for my liking. As I turned back to the house, my eye was drawn up towards the front bedroom. Unusually, the curtains were drawn open.

And there, standing in the window, was Bageye staring coldly at me and the departing car.

Saturday night came without my being pressed by my father for any details about my curious encounter with the white man in the car. He'd have to have witnessed it. But, then again, perhaps he hadn't. I'd read that sometimes a thing is so alien to the beholder that their brain is scrambled and they just can't see it. It made perfect sense; otherwise, surely, Bageye would have said something.

My brother and I prepared for the bout principally by taking the precaution not to eat, or if it had to be done then only snacking on something light, like scrambled eggs. We'd both witnessed the horror of what might happen to an unfortunate soul if landed with a blow to the belly before he'd had time to let his food digest.

A makeshift boxing ring had been erected in the middle of the social club behind the Catholic church. A dozen circular tables were dotted around the hall. Each one seated about five or six people, mostly the boys and their fathers, and perhaps a couple of friends. Of course Bageye was blissfully (and thankfully) ignorant of this fight night, so we could not have had a table to ourselves and were orphaned for the night. Brooksy arranged for Milton and me to be accommodated at the table of a set of dapper old-timers, some of who were rumoured to be boxing scouts. We didn't give it much thought but, in a way, our temporary attachment (or 'couching' as Jamaicans say) to these Irish scouts was a reflection of a larger truth: as one of the few Caribbean families around we were appendages to the bigger Irish story on Farley Hill.

Almost everyone in the club had on a suit and a glass of Guinness or shot of whisky in hand. As well as the scorecards giving the order of the bouts, the tables were decorated with little pads of betting slips. There'd never been a boxing event in the hall before, and, though I couldn't be sure, it seemed to me that all the adults, puffing on fat cigars probably for the first time, were playing at being a boxing audience.

That night I was matched against Martin Shannon. It was going to be a relatively easy fight. Because, though Martin had all the right moves, he rarely risked getting close enough to land a punch. His approach was an elaborate type of shadow boxing. He didn't transmit blows: he only received them. But more unnerving than this charade was the fact of his permanent cold and running nose.

I allowed Martin first pick of the shiny new, blood-red boxing gloves. In any event, I preferred the worn, tan-coloured ones. Not because the leather might be cracked on the outside and the padding lumpy on the inside, but somehow they possessed a dignity lacking in the new ones.

As I ducked in through the ropes into the ring, I caught sight of Mr Synott. He gave me a sly thumbs-up and a wink. This, perhaps unintentional, reminder that I was duty bound to double his earnings introduced an unwelcome and undermining thought: *What would it be like to lose?* There was no chance, obviously, because points were only scored with blows to the head or torso. Martin's air-punching wouldn't count. But the sounding of the bell and seconds-out led me to consider how it was that I had never given any attention to the effect of my fists on other boys' faces – until now.

I found myself mirroring Martin's boxing style: we were both boxing each other's shadow. The one time that I did connect, snot shot out from Martin's nose onto my gloves, so that I was disinclined to throw any more punches. At the end of that round, when I'd barely sat down, the referee steamed over to me. He could not hide his disgust of our pitiable display of manhood. Above the noise of the crowd he roared: 'I'm gonna stop this farce if you don't buck your ideas up.' I stood up on the bell and inched towards my opponent. The whole thing seemed suddenly absurd. I lowered my guard but Martin was incapable of taking advantage of my lack of defence. Instead of punching, he clung to me in an awkward bear hug. Some sections of the audience began to laugh but I couldn't shake him off.

The laughter rang around the hall and eventually reached a group of boys who, having finished their bouts, stood by the exits, flushed with pride or disappointment. Milton was among them but his back was turned from the ring. He appeared to be talking to someone, but was obscured by the others. Had not Martin Shannon been locked onto me, I would have been undone by nervousness about the overwhelming certainty of the stranger's identity. Gradually the group thinned, and as the remaining curtain of boys parted, my father was revealed. He made damn sure I'd seen him.

I don't recall how many seconds or minutes passed thereafter before I became aware of the sound of whimpering. It must have been Martin. Finally, the referee pulled me away roughly. And to my amazement, Martin Shannon was sprawled out on the canvas, his face covered in blood and snot.

It was the last bout of the night. After the winner's announcement, Billy Brooks signalled that we should remain in the ring. We were joined by all of the others who'd been on the bill that night. Once we thirty boys were assembled, Brooksy spoke though the microphone and invited the crowd to show their appreciation. Finally, he took a bag filled with sixpences – a month's worth of our weekly subscriptions to the boxing club. He reached into the bag and by the handful showered the ring with sixpences. The boys leapt into the air to catch the coins and darted around the ring, picking up the rest from the canvas. Despite the sight of Bageye and his stony look of disapproval, Milton and I dived into the melee to grab our share.

Our father was waiting for us outside afterwards. Given that he'd uncovered our deception, Bageye wasn't as angry as we'd expected, though he was scornful of Billy Brooks's generosity: 'Chicken feed. You see how it start? You go in there kill yourself; the big man place dem bet, and in the end you lef' with chicken feed.'

We walked back slowly through the night. The cold air on our skins was a relief after all the overheating from the exertions: the fighting in the ring and the undignified scramble at the end. Walking home under the blanket of stars, and guided by our father, there was a kind of harmony, a perfection that would have been spoilt if anyone had spoken. We walked on in silence. But just before we reached the house, Bageye stopped and addressed us both, breaking the spell: 'You better make the most of tonight, you know, 'cause all of this foolishness gwan finish when you start private school. No boxing, no football, no athletics, no cricket. Not one t'ing the Englishman expect of the black boy you gwan give him. You understan'? Not a t'ing.'

Shift Work

'POVERTY IS A HELL OF a thing,' said Mum. She sat at the kitchen table with a pen and paper. She was trying to write a letter but struggling at the same time to draw up a list of people she owed money to: the milkman, the council, Mrs Hannah . . . She read them out, saying either: 'This one can wait,' or 'That one need pay.' She didn't want the bailiff knocking on the door, she said, so the rent absolutely had to be paid. None of us joined in as it wasn't really a conversation: Blossom was just talking. Going down the list, she must have registered some worry on our faces because she brightened: 'So long as rent pay, you have a roof over your head. You have two potatoes and your belly full. What more you need?'

She put the list to one side and returned to the letter but had barely got beyond the first line when the knocking on the front door interrupted her thoughts. 'Ah, who that now?' We all looked at each other. Nobody had any idea. We could usually work out from the heaviness or urgency of the knocking whether it was somebody to be avoided. The tapping was gentler than expected but it didn't stop us worrying. Saturday mornings was most likely to be the milkman but no one could remember hearing the milk crates or the electric-powered float. When they knocked again we panicked. Everyone scarpered, mostly out into the garden. I wasn't quick enough and Blossom pulled me back. 'Go check it out,' she whispered. 'Look first.'

I sank to my hands and knees and started crawling down the hallway. Normally, if there was somebody at the door, their outline would fill the frame of the frosted glass. There didn't seem to be anybody. I reached the front room and made my way to the bay window and pulled back the netting a crack in the corner. With her back pressed to the wall beside the front door, like someone sheltering from a blustery wind, was the creditor we dreaded the most: the Blundell's woman. She stretched out her arm and with her pen lifted the door knocker and let it fall. She tried a couple more times and, when no one answered, moved away. I crawled back out of the living room. I'd made it halfway down the hallway when I heard behind me the sickening sound of the lid to the letter box being lifted, and when I turned my eyes met those of the Blundell's woman peering through the hole.

More than the sight of her, it was Bageye's voice in my head, telling me to 'get up off your knees' which propelled me to my feet and back towards the front door. I unlocked the door. The Blundell's woman was a blonde who always wore make-up, and always, in all weathers, wore high heels and a black mackintosh with a belt pulled tightly around her waist. I felt a little queer and flushed in her presence. She drew you in but repulsed you at the same time: she went from being, in my mind, a model for a clothes catalogue to a warden in a women's prison.

Thankfully, the Blundell's woman was not one for

small talk. Her nose was buried in the thick black ledger, brimful of debtors' pages. Blundell Bros was the biggest department store in town and had featured in all our lives ever since the move to Farley Hill when Bageye's spar, Patterson, had co-signed for him to get credit to furnish the empty house. Blundell's, our mother always said, were 'too nice' to us because as well as providing three-piece suites, beds and wardrobes, they also lent money; you were 'never done pay them back' and like tapeworms, would 'never get rid-a them'. When the money we owed got down to a few pounds, the Blundell's woman would suddenly appear.

She flicked through to our entry in the ledger and, glancing briefly in my direction so as not to lose the page, asked: 'Mummy at home?' I shook my head. 'Really?' She looked up over the rim of her glasses, and then took them off for a better look. After a few seconds I felt the heat coursing through my body, and she winked at me as if I had somehow given away the secret of a schoolboy's crush. Stepping closer and peering beyond, over my shoulder, she mouthed: *She in the back?* Despite being determined to resist I found my head nodding. I suppose it didn't matter because even as I was nodding Blossom appeared. Perhaps Mum had witnessed my betrayal, but I was grateful that she didn't pass comment.

I left them on the doorstep. The Blundell's woman was laughing with Mum as if the two of them were best friends. Their voices hushed for a while and became more serious and formal, and Blossom eventually closed the front door. When she came back into the kitchen, I thought she looked a little ashamed,

216

as though she had started smoking again or something. She sat down immediately at the table, found a pen and tried to pick up from the point she had left off from writing before the Blundell's woman had knocked.

The only letters I'd known Mum to write in her lovely italic handwriting were to her family – a rump of five adult siblings and her mother, who lived together in a big house on Harcourt Street, on the other, residential, side of town. It wasn't strange – the living arrangement – that's just the way it was. In fact, Blossom and Bageye had also spent months, maybe a year, there when she first came to England, before moving out to Farley Hill. Individually, the family members were fine: collectively, they reminded me of Mrs Ayres on one of her off days.

For as long as I could remember, Blossom had written regularly to them. At first, they'd been responsive. Once, a pair of the Adams men turned up at the house after a report that Bageye had raised a hand to their sister. Bageye was absent when they arrived and I remember how, in their frustration, they'd twisted the thick curtain in the living room, strangling it in place of my father's neck. But largely, Blossom felt abandoned by the Harcourt Street mob to the man whom she'd married against their will and wisdom. In the last few months, Harcourt Street had ceased to return her letters and she suspected that the pleas for help that she'd painstakingly and humbly composed had remained unopened. She might just as well have written to Father Christmas.

Blossom made several attempts now to continue with this new letter before finally screwing up the paper.

'I thrown corn,' she said emphatically, 'but I don't call no fowl.' She was happy to ask for help, but refused to beg.

The following week more hatboxes arrived, and, though she worked conscientiously on sticking the feathers to the hats, the pile never seemed to diminish. After several deliveries, a bewildering maze of boxes was permanently jammed in the living room from wall to wall and floor to ceiling. Feathers were strewn across the floor like a chicken coop after a visit from a fox. But it was only when we stopped and thought about the lack of expected complaints from Bageye that we realised we had hardly seen him for a month. Since the entrance exam he'd been working all the shifts he could get – day and night and sometimes back to back.

There was noticeably more bickering in his absence. It started with the missing ruler (we never did fully accept Bageye's insistence on 'rule'). Milton had stood up in front of the whole school at assembly to receive the twelve-inch metallic ruler after coming first in a maths competition. He held out for a miraculous return but the ruler was never seen again, and in time was forgotten. The same was true of the mystery over the vanishing sheets of brown paper that Blossom used when steam-ironing the laundry. But when the weighing scales disappeared from the kitchen, Blossom started to get seriously worried. It might be the return of a duppy, she argued, or some other devil work. Her alarm deepened when perfectly cut-out two-inch squares of the brown paper started turning up around the house. And finally her anxiety shot off the scales when Milton found one of the tiny sheets of paper wrapped up neatly in the style of a sachet of Beechams Powders. Inside the sachet was what looked like a mixture of tea leaves and tobacco. 'My bad eye a-dance,' Blossom immediately began to wail. 'I see trouble in this house tonight.'

Our mother had an eye that often twitched, or the skin just beneath the eyelid at any rate. I'd lost count of the number of times she'd announce gravely: 'My bad eye a-dance.' All her life the mystery of this dancing eye had stayed with her. Whenever her bad eye was on the move it brought on an unshakeable feeling of foreboding. Through her bad eye she was forever seeing 'trouble in this house tonight'. Blossom might place an index finger on the skin under the eye and stop the twitching perhaps, but that sense of foreboding never left her.

She emptied the sachet down the loo and flushed the chain more times than was necessary. 'Ganja,' whispered Selma. Blossom returned to the bathroom several times to check that the ganja had not risen back to the top of the toilet bowl. She was continually on the move now. She shot around the house, opening doors and drawers, lifting up cushions and rifling through pockets in coats. She couldn't stop. There was a frightening urgency about the way she moved around, turning the house upside down – until suddenly she froze. In the furthest reaches of the airing cupboard she had found the missing weighing scales. For a moment she caught her breath and bit her lip so hard I feared it would bleed. She began weeping as well as wailing.

'Anybody see my cross! Anybody see my cross!'

The Lord God never gave you a burden that you

couldn't carry, Mum believed, but this cross was too much. Her distress was painful to watch. Most of us, including me, started to cry. I didn't really know why, except that some great calamity had obviously befallen us but Blossom couldn't speak of it: she could only wail and pray. Her prayers were pitiful.

And just as suddenly, it seemed, she stopped. Blossom placed the weighing scales carefully on the kitchen table as if it was a precious antique. She dried her tears, smiled faintly, sat down at the table and waited. She was still in the same position a couple of hours later when Bageye crashed through the front door with his young spar Maraj in tow.

'Whoa!' Maraj reared back out of the living room at the sight of the hatboxes. 'How much hat one man can wear? You have hat for me? Where is my hat?'

'Is mostly woman hat,' answered Bageye. 'Plant your backside down, man, I soon come. If you cyann' find seat, find yourself a hat.' Bageye broke into a smile but then seemed to remember where he was, and tried, not quite successfully, to swallow it. He bounded up the stairs two steps at a time. We heard him rummaging in the airing cupboard. Descending the stairway slowly soon after, every step was a step towards coming to terms with a secret now revealed. The vestiges of a smile that remained in his eyes were tinged with disappointment. He entered the kitchen and made straight for the table and snapped up the weighing scales in a manner, if not quite of the winning captain on a team picking up the trophy, then close to it. Blossom may have thought her wait was over, that she was entitled to an explanation, but she was wrong.

Instead Bageye made some dry comment about the need for Blossom to look for other work because, though he was a man with long patience: 'The hats, man. The hats . . .' Bageye was so disturbed he could hardly speak but his wife had better understand that he would be recapturing the living room in one week. He was 'gwan tek it back, yes!' It started off as a passing remark but Bageye was goaded by Mum's silence to bring to her attention other shortcomings he'd noticed recently. He'd barely warmed up when Maraj popped his head through the strips of curtain to see what was going on.

Whenever Maraj came into a room he always left it colder than when he first arrived. Only after he'd gone would normal room temperature be restored. For a door-to-door salesman this might have been a problem. But then Maraj should not have been a salesman. He was extremely handsome: a tall Trinidadian Indian with long black hair and shiny skin; women fluttered about him when he was near. But there was nothing warm about Maraj. Trying, as he did, to befriend us kids always made it worse. Perhaps we were prejudiced by the stories we heard about him. As a door-to-door salesman, Maraj went around all the West Indian houses with a suitcase of clothes and sold on credit. He was doing enough to get by but then one day the brethren he shared a flat with, a man by the name of 'So and So', took off with his suitcase of clothes and shipped back to Jamaica. Maraj always vowed to 'push a knife in so far' into So and So's belly if he ever caught up with him. It was all talk, they said, but, a little while back, one of the fellas had run across So and So (things hadn't worked out

221

for him in Jamaica, and he was back, not in Luton but in Ipswich) and the fella said it pained him to look at So and So because his face was spoilt by a red-raw scar that ran from his ear to his lip.

'I find a hat,' said Maraj. 'You want see?' Bageye hadn't finished with Blossom yet, he let her know, but allowed Maraj to take his arm and coax him from the kitchen. He pulled Bageye through the strip curtain and shook him, as a corner man might a dazed fighter, forcibly, trying to revive the old Bageye – the amused and amusing one that he had come to the house with just minutes ago. They tumbled back into the living room and slammed the door loudly enough for everyone to realise that it was big people's time and only a fool or madman would dare to disturb them. Almost immediately the sweet fug of the special cigarettes escaped from under the doorway and hung about in a thin cloud in the hallway. It was a smell associated with the night yet it wasn't even midday, and it roused and riled our mother in a way that Bageye had failed to. She looked to each of us in turn. There was a question in that searching expression and each of us shook our heads in answer to what she was about to do. Blossom shot out of her chair, walked briskly down the hallway and barged in on Bageye and Maraj.

They must have been surprised because there was hardly any sound apart from Maraj's rumbling snort as he tried to stop himself from giggling. Someone, probably Maraj, pushed the door carefully behind her. There was still no shouting, only murmuring after several minutes had passed. All of us kids eventually positioned ourselves on the other side of the door.

Bizarrely, though no one else had come into the house, there seemed to be an extra voice in the living room – one that we didn't recognise, insisting that 'everyt'ing cool, man'. It wasn't just that our ears had never grown accustomed to the gentle and soothing qualities of our father's voice but that the tone of intimacy and tenderness was directed at Blossom. She wasn't listening. She emerged fuming more than when she had gone in, and in no time swept us all up and out of the house and marched us to the rec.

For weeks afterwards, whenever anyone asked me how I was, I'd always respond, either in my head or actually, depending who they were: 'Yes, everyt'ing cool, man.' And I kept my ears peeled for any suggestion between my parents that Bageye was about to speak to Blossom with that same tenderness, but he never did. It seemed even less likely than before, and I began to recall how unlikely it had been in the first place, and wondered whether we had actually just imagined it, the way people imagined God speaking to them, or their cats.

But the first sign that things were different, that our circumstances had changed, came with the broken biscuits. There was still the ritual of assembling around the box and taking turns to pick out a custard cream or jammy dodger before settling on the dry and crumbly remains at the very end. But now we only had to wait a week, rather than a month, for the next box of broken biscuits. Neither did Bageye stiffen up when I mentioned to him, as Blossom had instructed, that it was only a month or so before term began and both Milton and I needed uniforms. And then one Saturday we drove to Bernard's junk shop and slapped down cash on the counter for a new piece of lino.

The only downside to Bageye's new-found ease with money was the near-constant presence of Maraj. The Maraj who'd come to the house the month before must have been an impostor because soon the real Maraj raised his head, and it wasn't pleasant: Maraj wasn't just walnut dark. All the light had been sucked out of him. The hatboxes in the living room went and Maraj took their place. He was one of them fellas, Mum complained, who 'turn up beg a glass a water and just move them arse inside. Get them to move now? Which part? You have to burn them out.' More worrying for Blossom was that he'd wormed his way into Bageye 'like a jigga in the man heel'.

Maraj slept on the settee in the living room and never got up till the afternoon. Blossom asked him about the odd hours he seemed to work, considering he was supposed to be a door-to-door salesman, and he replied: 'I don't business with that again.' When he did emerge he never seemed able to shake off the heavy sleep and there were permanent dark patches under his eyes. He seemed to us like a man on the run. Maraj could spend hours just flicking his penknife open and shut and occasionally freeing a speck of dirt from under a fingernail. Other than that he'd lounge about the place until such time when he'd announce he was leaving now 'to do a little business with Bageye'. The two men would roll back in once everyone was in bed, and the pattern would repeat itself the next day.

Perhaps Maraj just liked company because he got upset if he came into a room (even the bathroom) where you already were and you tried to leave – though he never asked any questions or volunteered anything about himself. He was about as sociable as a cat. And nobody was surprised when we got up one morning and peered into the living room to find that he was gone.

It was about this time that the old rancour started to eat its way back into Bageye's soul. Mention St Columba's College and he'd start cussing about how Mum was just 'following dem Adams people'. Parts of our school uniforms still needed to be bought, but if you couldn't hurry him, you also couldn't second-guess him. One evening Bageye came home with a pair of leather briefcases for me and Milton. They were the most beautiful things I'd ever seen. At least half a dozen times during the day I gave in to the compulsion for one last inspection. Carefully turning the key in the lock, easing the buckle from the catch, I'd open up my case and inhale that lovely new leather smell, and I'd think to myself: *Yes, man. Everyt'ing cool.*

Bageye itched to see the briefcases put to their important use, and while there was still time he arranged to borrow one 'jus' till school start'. Milton and I made a calendar and counted down the days. Nobody much complained now about the mutton and pigtail soup which previously would only have gone down our throats if force-fed. Especially now, with that date in striking distance, Blossom didn't need to explain that we had to watch our pennies. Still, it grieved me to see my mother having to set out early with the bag of washing for the laundry well before Mrs Ayres or anyone got there and started making noises about her hogging the tumble dryers.

There was, of course, nobility in grief. You clung to it together with the blanket as you turned over in a half-dream in the comfort of your bed and listened to the click of the front door as Mum tiptoed away with the wet laundry.

It was on one of those days, in the early hours, soon after Blossom had left, that Bageye came to the door and summoned me to his room. Several sheets of brown paper were stacked on the bed. I noticed Milton's ruler there too, as well as the weighing scales. Bageye scrutinised my face and followed my gaze to the open sweet bag full of ganja beside the scales. I had no time to work out whether to be ignorant or knowing.

Bageye made no reference to what was going on but he obviously wanted my help in preparing the sachets. The first task was to halve the brown sheets of paper again and again to make the squares. He demonstrated, folding a sheet and then sliding the ruler along the crease, slicing as he did so. When I'd made a dozen squares, he took the bag and, pinching a clump of ganja, dropped some onto each square. He did it all by eye. The scales remained unused even though he was worried about the amounts. Each time he'd inspect the little pile of ganja on the square of paper and ask: 'What you think? It share too heavy?'

We agreed that more was more than less and left it at that. It was best not to ask too many questions. Bageye recognised that there was a time for questions and a time for action – for doing something or being someone. My father was not a man for endless reflection: he was a doer and a dreamer. That much was clear to me even at that age. Once we settled on the amount the rest was up to him for he was skilled, with his nimble fingers, at turning the squares into sachets, making an oblong and folding one end of the paper into the other. He went to the wardrobe and took one of the briefcases. Thankfully, it was Milton's. Bageye opened the case and one at a time deposited the individual sachets with great care in the front pouch. Afterwards, he brushed his fingers together. It was a funny gesture. The whole procedure had a nagging familiarity to it. Eventually it came to me: Bageye's actions were just like Blossom's when she prepared a tray of cupcakes for the oven. He closed the lid gently as she might have closed the oven door.

He locked the briefcase with the tiny key and told me to go and get dressed. 'Put on your new school clothes,' he shouted as I hurried out the door. I suppose it was odd but at the time I didn't think anything of it. You were so used to not asking questions that after a while the questions didn't even arise. Even so, it was a shame to be putting on the uniform before starting school properly. It spoilt the idea a little but I tried to push my disappointment to one side by getting dressed really quickly, and dashing back to my father's room, to present myself for inspection. Bageye was already downstairs. Holding the front door open he shouted: 'Come, let's go.' My father made little mention of the uniform other than to say: 'Fit good.' And when he gave me the briefcase to hold on to, I was determined to be the very best holder of briefcases there'd ever been.

I took up my position in the passenger seat while Bageye lifted the bonnet and removed the layers of newspaper that had lain as a precaution on top of the engine overnight – a trick learnt from Joe Burns – to keep out the dew. It worked a treat, as expected, though it was still possible to register the delight on Bageye's face when the engine started first time.

Anxious was the very first stop. He didn't look so honoured when he opened the door to his flat.

'Who dead?' he mumbled. 'Must be someone dead.'

Anxious was so tired he had to prop himself up along the wall as he led the way to the living room.

'What time you have?' He grabbed Bageye's wrist and yet struggled to make sense of where the hands were pointing. 'But wait, you don't suppose for visit someone in the middle of the night.'

'Sunrise from time, man,' Bageye murmured.

Anxious's housekeeping had not improved since our last visit. Bageye took a handkerchief and, pulling up a chair, flicked the dust from the seat before sitting down.

'You gwan too extra.' Anxious cast a weary eye in my direction. 'So who dead? You know? Your daddy nah seem to know.'

Bageye beckoned me over and pointed to the ground. I was to leave the briefcase behind and go and wait for him in the hallway. Noticeably he said 'hallway', not the kitchen or dining room. It was his way of saying that if I paid attention there was a chance I might learn an important lesson. I could hear him opening the case and snatches of the conversation – mostly bluff and bluster over the difference between the cost of the sachet and its value.

'Just one?' Anxious joked. 'Look like you have plenty.'

'How much you want one time?'

'Let me hold two.'

The lock to the briefcase sprang open again. 'Two, you say?'

'One little one nah even gwan touch the side,' said Anxious. 'But how much it retail?'

'Ten for the two.'

'Ten in new money?'

'Nah must.'

'How much dat in old money?' asked Anxious.

It'd been over a year since decimalisation but Anxious was still working in guineas and shillings. Bageye didn't sound too sure. He made up a figure that was way off.

'Dat sound about right,' said Anxious.

On the way out I just about held off until we reached the car before whispering to Bageye the mistake that Anxious had made, paying almost twice as much in the new money. I imagined Bageye would have been as excited as I was about the error. He wasn't. He insisted I calculate the difference between what had been received and what Anxious should reasonably have been expected to hand over. When I'd finished, he asked: 'What would you do?'

'I suppose you should—' I started to say, but Bageye cut me off.

'I didn't ask "should". I asked what you would do.'

My answer wasn't quick enough. Bageye counted out the difference in change, added a bit more, and ordered me to hurry back with it to the flat before Anxious was reunited with his bed. For quite a while – after I got back to the car – I couldn't look at my father because he couldn't look at me.

Bageye pulled up at Joe Burns's next, up at High

Town. Again I was confined to the hallway. Perhaps because Joe's women were still asleep, the voices of the two men were hushed and hurried. Joe did not have any cash. He went into the kitchen and came back with some magazines and a plastic bag filled with frozen meat. 'You tek me for idiot,' said Bageye sourly. But Joe held his hands up and asked something like whether my father actually needed money or was he 'looking supplementary benefit'? Bageye was too disgusted to give him a straight answer. Some kind of exchange must have occurred though because Bageye snatched the bag of meat. Joe, as we say, didn't dig his attitude. Things had not been the same between them since the trip to St Albans for the entrance exam. Some hurt or resentment was carried over on both sides. It seemed at the back of everything though it was never expressed. It was pitiful in a way because if my father really loved any human being then I suspect it was Joe. But though neither relished the breach, neither seemed to know how, or was willing, to repair it. Joe told my father he didn't like the set-up. Why, he wondered, had Bageye brought me along.

'And why him in the school uniform?'

'Him just a-try it on.'

Joe told him it didn't make sense. He was particularly troubled by the fact that Bageye had given me the briefcase to carry. At this point Bageye told him to lower his voice a little, but Joe refused. The real worry, he said, was Maraj. 'The man all over town asking for you. You must know what you a-deal with.' Bageye mumbled some angry response which I strained to hear. All I could really make out was Joe's final warning: 'You steppin' in shit, my friend.'

When Bageye came into the hallway his eyes were ablaze. Joe followed, making sounds that, without actually saying so, expressed his reluctance to see Bageye depart. He had some Marvel comics he wanted to give me to add to my collection. My father put out his hand, blocking Joe. 'Him soon a college man. The boy nah want comic. Is book we want.'

'C'mon now, man,' said Joe. 'This between you and me. It nah have for involve the boy.'

Bageye ignored his friend. 'Let me ask the boy.' His voice was taut and serious, as he turned towards me: 'The man is giving you this.' He spoke slowly as if for the benefit of someone who didn't understand English. 'You want it?' I did not want to catch Joe's eye. I lowered my gaze, and shook my head.

It wasn't long before we reached Mrs Knight's. 'End of the line,' Bageye reassured me. We walked in the back way. Several men were sitting around the table – the usual crowd. As soon as we came through they shouted, with a mix of delight and amusement: 'Chargehand!'

My father was often the chargehand, overseeing the poker table at Mrs Knight's. Blossom had told us this more than once but the way she said it, it never sounded complimentary: 'But him never tek charge. Is pure chance him tek.' The men were salty in their talk. They paused when they saw me.

'But wait, a–who dat?' one of them asked.

'Look like John Brown.'

'Likkle Lord Fauntleroy,' said another.

'No, man, is Bageye son dat?'

'You lie! Bageye, is your son dat?'

The teasing was a little too blunt. My father didn't appreciate it. 'Onoo too ignorant,' he said. 'Why you don't climb back up in your tree.' But his comments only seemed to spur them on.

'Tell you dah trut' him look a little Bageyeish.'

'Aye, sir, is Bageye son for true.'

On and on they went. Bageye tried to make light of it and eventually the joke expired, but I felt and fully understood perhaps for the first time that he had ordered me to wear the new private school uniform to show me off; and more importantly, that my father had always considered that 'Bageye' was a term of abuse. It was a fleeting thought that passed, thankfully, as quickly as a fast-moving cloud over the sun.

The fellas had been up all night, and the room was warm from all the talk and from the smell of whisky and Guinness on their stale breath. It added to the overpowering fug of the sweet and sickly ganja vapours. There was something charming about the way they passed round the long and thickly packed cigarette. It made me think of Red Indians in a circle puffing on their peace pipe.

Bageye told me to leave the briefcase with him and go and find somewhere to sit in another room. I felt my way through the dark hallway to the dining room and slumped in a deep leather chair. I must have dozed off because, soon it seemed, my father was shaking me and ordering me to follow him quick time out the house. Having made the urgent getaway, he sat in the car for some time in the morning gloom before starting the engine.

'I don't have no luck,' is all he said.

★

You could tell it was Maraj from a hundred yards away just by the way he moved. Maraj, they used to say, had a 'prison walk' from all the times he'd been inside and forced to take exercise in the quad. He took no pleasure in walking. As we passed him you could see he was sweating. Strands of silky hair stuck to his face, and he clasped a big brown package too tightly under his arms – if he'd squeezed it only a little more then the entire contents would have spilt out onto the street. There were no alleyways on Farley Hill for Maraj to lurk in but that's probably where he'd have preferred to have been rather than continually circling the block having to pretend that he'd just arrived.

Maraj caught up with the car as it neared the house. He grasped the door handle and attempted to get into the car before Bageye had even properly brought it to a stop. I was told to go inside and no sooner had I stepped out than Maraj jumped into my seat – the way we did when the music stopped for musical chairs.

My thoughts turned to Bruce Wayne as I walked in my new uniform back towards the house. Bruce Wayne had a gift for changing out of his Batman outfit back into his ordinary clothes, always in the nick of time. I was troubled by the dilemma of how to get out of my uniform and back into my house clothes undetected.

Though nothing had been said, Blossom, Milton and I had all spent weeks imagining starting at the new school: the splendour and dignified solemnity of preparing for it; the transformation of putting on the uniform for the very first time; removing the neatly folded shirts from the cellophane packaging, taking out the pins that attached the sleeves to the back; extracting the cardboard that preserved the shape of the collar; lifting out the spanking new shoes from their boxes and tying the laces firmly in a double bow. All had been rehearsed in our minds.

When I reached the front door, trying to straighten my crumpled jacket, shirt and tie, Blossom opened the door. Her face – already primed for disappointment – plunged further into such depths of pity that I had to avert my eyes. I wasn't to blame. She knew that. But still, why had I put up no resistance? One of my mother's sayings – 'Only a coward let the other man fight for him' – rang in my ears, although her lips didn't move.

It was almost a relief to hear Bageye barging into the house. He was on a sudden mission. 'The book, where is the book?' he asked. Bageye meant the family allowance book which our mother guarded. We all knew – though Bageye only suspected – that she hadn't cashed any payments for several months now to help with the first term's school fees. 'Where is the book?' he growled in a voice that was louder now, on the fringes of anger. Blossom didn't answer and when he saw her looking heavenwards, he charged upstairs to the bedroom and began thrusting open doors and cupboards. Blossom put on an overcoat, though she didn't leave the house. Pretty soon we could hear Bageye slowly descending the stairs. There was no escape from his imminent arrival.

Bageye stormed into the kitchen. He pulled open kitchen drawers, checked under pots and pans and even inside the tins where we kept the sugar and flour.

He stopped abruptly, as if noticing Mum for the first time. An idea was dawning on him. 'Why you wearing the coat?' Blossom didn't answer. He told her to take off the coat. She refused. Bageye patted down the sides of her coat until he found what he was looking for. Blossom turned her head away. She knew better than to put up a fight. Her husband pulled open the coat. He unpicked some of the stitches that Blossom must have only recently made. He ripped the lining of the coat until the hole was big enough for him to reach in and pull out the prize: the family allowance book.

Bageye was not triumphant. He looked drained and relieved. But even as he counted the uncashed pages of the book, the pleasure drained from his face as the bigger truth began to assert itself that this relief, though welcome, would be temporary. Our mother had to understand that he didn't want to do it: he had to do it and she had forced him to act in this way. It sounds unlikely but he was convincing and when Bageye spoke you could see what Blossom meant when she'd later ask herself or anyone within earshot: 'Don't know why I let that man brainwash me.'

We stuck around, I suppose, to see whether Mum would risk changing her mind and try to wrestle the book back from him. But when we were sure that the surrender was complete and irreversible we headed off for the rec.

It was remarkable how, after a couple of hours messing around at the rec, on the fringes of the bluebell wood, you could forget all of the details of what had gone on previously in the house and focus instead on the important task of gathering enough acorns for the acorn fight against the boys from Priestley's just a few streets away. Maybe it was because we were hunting for the enemy in among the silver birch and maple trees that when my father appeared, walking fast on the outskirts of the wood, I decided to follow him – at a distance. I could not recall Bageye ever walking in the woods. And even more bizarrely, I had to run to try to keep up and in a little while I'd lost sight of him. When I found him again, he was crouched down behind a tree and some bushes. He had a trowel in his hand, digging out some earth. Beside the hole was a brown package. It was the same one we'd seen Maraj with earlier. Bageye looked up as I approached. He didn't look alarmed. Quite the opposite, as if he'd been expecting me. He put the package in the hole. It didn't fit. He dug some more and tried again: 'What you t'ink?' he asked. 'A good spot?'

The Package

It was gone. no matter how long Bageye stared at the spot on the cold ground where the parcel ought to be, it failed to materialise. Just two nights previously my father and I had buried the package under a bush in the woods, ten paces from the perimeter fence, but now, after almost half an hour of searching, all of the bushes started to look the same. We had been so careful. It was not possible: it made no sense. For it to be true then the impossible had happened. But it was true, and the time was close when Bageye would be forced to admit that he was in the midst of a catastrophe. Still, he was not yet reconciled to its permanent loss. The pending disaster called for all of his powers of concentration.

I don't think my father ignored me deliberately. He seemed to be trying to outfox himself, looking away, and looking back in the hope that it might magically reappear. He approached the spot from a different direction. Still nothing. He paced to the high metal fence that backed onto the motorway and tried once more, this time varying the speed of his approach. He came up short yet again. Bageye slapped his thighs as they began to stiffen. The alarm had induced a kind of catatonia. I had never seen my father panic: it was not his style. If he could just loosen up, act naturally, walk more casually in a 'This hasn't happened so why should I be worrying?' kind of way, then it might just be possible.

Bageye had posted me as lookout on the edge of the wood. I stood to attention, trapped inside a hooded parka; I could hardly see out and was not entirely sure what to be looking out for. I was, in any event, more concerned about the open-toed sandals that I'd chosen poorly and the unseen creatures of the night that lurked underfoot in the damp grass. The one thing I could see, though, was the first signs of sweat breaking through the balding circle at the back of my father's head. The package − amounting to a year's wages, maybe more − was not there. I knew nothing of the true value of its contents or its magical properties. I knew only that it involved the weighing scales, kept in the airing cupboard, and that its great bulk − the size of a proper Bible − when broken up into small pieces would be sold.

Bageye looked over to me and I imagined a cold slither of hate sliding across his heart. Whatever had possessed him to let me, a boy of ten, decide where to hide the package in the first place? Just forty-eight hours before, we had scouted the wood looking for a suitable hiding place. And when after half an hour Bageye still hesitated over the choices, he'd sought my opinion, for good luck. My father now kept up a mantra as he scoured the ground, muttering to himself something that sounded like: 'Whatever possess me let the boy decide?' If he'd bothered to reflect then Bageye would have arrived at the simple truth: that it was his nature. As Mum repeatedly said: 'That man like to take chance.'

Like every great gambler Bageye was addicted to

losing, to the thrill of the real possibility of betting his shirt and forfeiting absolutely everything. It had always been so. Tonight he was well on the road to succeeding. He hocked noisily and the slight glance in my direction told me he was disappointed in himself for spitting in front of his son, more so because he was loath to use his newly starched kerchief. He bent low for a few blades of grass to wipe the spittle from his chin, all the while muttering: 'Madness. Must be madness take me.'

I was determined both to cry and not to cry. I clenched my jaw to push back the tears.

'Never mind,' said Bageye about the parcel, 'dog must be gone with it. Better it dog than the Blues. Anyhow, Babylon get a-hold of it, you could-a kiss this arse goodbye.' He commanded: 'Stop your noise!' as the beginnings of a cry formed at the back of my throat.

We had come prepared with a trowel. Bageye stabbed hard at the earth one last time with extraordinary venom. He hit a large stone or rock and the trowel struck with such force that the handle splintered. I recoiled, but not from the violence; after all, such acts were not uncommon. Just this morning, my father had filled a pot of water and not being able to remove it easily from the sink – when the demon entered his soul – he had pulled up the pot with such anger that he caught and ripped off the cold water tap; water had shot out like an erupting geyser all over the kitchen. No, I recoiled towards the darkness of the woods because I did not want Bageye to see that, through some strange, involuntary act, the insides of my trousers had become suddenly and inexplicably wet.

239

Bageye had obviously had enough of this particular farce. And who could blame him? He walked off now out of the woods without me; I stood rooted to the spot, not knowing whether I had permission to follow. After a few minutes my father returned, stopped at the edge of the clearing and shouted: 'Come if you coming.' It was all I could do to stop myself from tripping as I ran, struggling to keep up with him down the steep wooded path to Ferndale Road. As we approached the corner shop, lit up in an ethereal beauty of neon against the coming night, Bageye pulled up with no prompting from me and pointedly not looking back, said in an even voice: 'You have anything to eat since morning?' He did not wait for an answer. Bageye moved on into the shop and emerged a short while later, chucking a bag of crisps in my direction.

'Stop your noise,' he called out again, but this time almost tenderly, at the sound of me revving up once more.

Some men, when they take a beating, drop to their knees in prayer. My father's answer was to be found not at the altar but at the poker table – at Mrs Knight's yard. Without saying anything to me I knew he had resolved to win back the loss of sales from the ganja package through a spectacular win at Mrs Knight's all-weekend poker game.

To get to Mrs Knight's the quickest solution would have been to scramble back up through the bushes and climb into the Mini estate but that would have meant retracing our steps. This was something Bageye simply could not do: it went against his code. Wet blades of grass had worked their way into the cuffs of Bageye's trouser legs and I resisted the urge to bend down and turn them out – just, just resisted. So that when I found myself on one knee and the heat of my father's gaze on the back of my head, I made to tighten the buckle on my sandal.

The pleasure of giving the crisps was not matched by a concomitant joy on Bageye's part of watching his son open the packet and munch his way through them. Walking and eating was an activity that Bageye had previously negatively ruled on. I couldn't remember the specificity of my father's ruling on it but there was likely to have been a ruling. 'Can I save them for later?' I asked and Bageye nodded approvingly.

Up Ferndale Road, it was then, and right into Longcroft Hill. Ferndale was one of those roads that mocked with its superior cars – the kinds of motors that Bageye would never be able to afford and so had to be passed at speed. The hill had been denuded of trees after complaints of mugging from the local tenants on the estate and those silver birches that remained stood at regular intervals silhouetted like sentinels in the cloudy night. They matched the silence that seemed to have taken root between my father and me. The longer it remained the more difficult it became to break. Eventually, he defaulted to his prime subject, at least as far as conversations with me were concerned: his wife.

'So what that woman have to say?'

I never had anything much to offer but my approach was the same as the one I used for Saturday-morning confession: get it over with as quickly as possible; make something up – not too controversial – and receive absolution. But my mind was still fixed on trying to visualise the missing package. I couldn't think of anything.

'What that woman have to say?' Bageye was more insistent.

Finally, I settled on the cupboard door in the kitchen that was nearly off its hinges.

'I think she's worried about the drop-down door,' I said.

'What about the drop-down door?'

In a voice as blithe as I could muster, I suggested that it needed fixing.

'Again? It fix already!' my father answered angrily.

We reached the Mini estate before he could grill me any more. The car was parked at the base of Longcroft Hill. A speck of rust broke away from the door's hinge as Bageye slid into the driver's seat. He turned to observe me manoeuvring into the passenger seat. I thought it wise not to consider the possible poor outcome of the door test. The thing closed with a pleasing thud and I turned as an ice-skater might at the end of his routine to scrutinise the scorecards for an expected perfect 10. But for once Bageye wasn't paying attention. He had turned halfway round to see out of the rear window. He released the handbrake and the car rolled back down the hill to the flat. Only then did he start the engine; he revved it up, took off and was quickly into third gear. 'Let we see if she make it all the way up.' My father's face took on a peculiar aspect, almost of contentedness, as we reached the top of the hill without having to change down a gear. 'You see what the car do? What you think is the reason for that?'

'Tuning,' I answered confidently.

'And what is tuning?'

It was not always wise to know as much as my father, so I feigned ignorance, and shrugged.

Bageye spoke earnestly: 'You tune an instrument to make sure it hit the right note. Y'understand?'

'Right.'

'Right. Same with car. You're not too small to know these things. One day you will thank me.'

I recognised my father's fondness for these impromptu lessons in life. I looked forward to them as rare moments of intimacy, even though they were often dispatches from a sometimes painful past. For instance, whenever the subject of education came up, my father would question the value of 'qualifications', attaching a certain degree of scorn to the word. Yet he felt sufficiently ambivalent about it to have been cajoled into saving to send us to private school, and every little bit of extra finance now, including what the package would have brought in, was supposed to pay for our first term.

Was it really necessary? 'No one learn me,' Bageye would add with familiar bitterness. But then again, if ever I suggested that the prospective private school was going to be too expensive, he would cut me off, saying firmly: 'Stop talk tripe, man. Not a t'ing more important than headucation.' When it came to schooling then my father was something of a fair-weather zealot. Bageye wasn't going to bequeath the legacy of his lack of learning to his children. That impulse for betterment lay behind the purchase of the most expensive item in the house: a full set of volumes of the *Encyclopaedia Britannica*, acquired from a travelling rep who knocked on our door one day.

But our father worried that after several months of payments for the encyclopaedias there were few signs of improvement in our overall intelligence. Once I overheard him joking with the fellas that his pickney were sub-standard. 'One or two might do something,' but the others were 'not even government issue'.

Bageye rarely panicked but if you really knew him, you'd know he was an anxious man. Not as anxious as Anxious but anxious nonetheless. His anxiety was most easily registered on his lips, fringed by a pencil-thin moustache, which quivered when troubled by a disturbing thought. I imagined him reflecting now on the unopened encyclopaedias, on his pickney's ungrateful bottomless bellies, on the whispering mother–child conspiracies when he awoke for the night shift, on the missing package in the woods, and on the curse of being a Negro. Bageye's foot slipped off the pedal and the car lurched and stalled. He added the kiss-me-arse car to the list, to the darkening mood that propelled him from it towards the house.

Forty-two Castlecroft Road had not known many periods of plenty. Each week Bageye moaned that there was 'only one wage coming in'. That time of grace, when the family could luxuriate in the possibilities of how the pounds might stretch, was extremely short. Essential house money, for food and clothes, was surrendered rather than volunteered, and Bageye made no secret that the surrender might at times be temporary. The missing package required immediate and direct action. The scale of the loss would need a change to his fortune of equal magnitude. For some reason Bageye evidently thought the answer might lie at 42 Castlecroft Road. He stormed through the hallway into the kitchen now, and pressed Mum for the house money for the second time in less than a week. 'Where is it?' he demanded.

'It finish,' answered his wife.

'Don't tell me lie, woman.'

My mother, who would never have made a spy, inadvertently looked over to the larder and gave away its hiding place. The flour jar's label had been switched with the sugar jar's in a weak attempt to throw Bageye off the scent from his regular reacquisition of money that would only have been handed over the night before; things would have gone badly had nothing been found. He snorted with a kind of embarrassed satisfaction that most of the money was still there.

All of us children took refuge in the hallway and hushed each other to silence, wishing Mum would do the same. But we heard her wondering aloud, at the upper register of her voice, as to why – now that he'd found what he was looking for – he was still in the house. If he'd had previous doubts about the wisdom of remaining, his mind was made up now.

Bageye opened the drop-down door and reached into the cupboard for a cloth and shoe brush. He bent and flicked off the grass from the turn-up on his trousers and made an extra slow shine of his shoes.

'What are you waiting for? Why you don't gwan about your business?' said Mum, struggling to keep her counsel. 'Yes, gwan to your bluefoot.'

There was a pause in the brushing. Bageye straightened like a blade emerging from a flick knife. He thrust out his neck from his collar and dared her to repeat herself. We children willed her not to but knew she could not resist. Of all the trigger words, 'bluefoot' – we'd worked out that this meant some kind of bad lady – was the worst.

'Yes, run to your bluefoot.'

A pot of rice had recently been set to boil on the stove and Bageye dropped the shoe brush now and picked up the pot.

'You wouldn't dare!' Mum screamed.

But before he had time to decide, Selma placed her hand on top of Bageye's arm and he lowered the pot onto the stove. The rest of us scrambled out of his way, away from Bageye's red-eyed retreat from the kitchen, and into the bathroom where sink taps were opened and run just short of overflowing and the toilet chain suffered a series of violent yanks.

A phoney quiet settled over the house as we all waited for him to go. Sometimes he would announce his departure with a loud slam, at other times you weren't sure whether he had left at all. After about ten minutes, the all-clear was sounded and, like the inoculated child who only cries out once the needle is successfully removed from her shoulder, the younger ones now began to weep.

Mum berated them gently for crying so easily. She found a piece of scrap paper and a pencil and began to write quickly and purposefully, all the while talking to herself but loud enough for everyone to hear.

'We need some Carnation milk. And better get some porridge oats too . . .'

She soothed us now as she so often did with the simple preparation of a shopping list. She entrusted me with the list and an envelope addressed to the manager of the Wavy Line.

'Oh, and if any change leave' – she smiled – 'you can get a box of broken biscuit.'

I didn't need to open the letter to know its contents. Inside was a note asking for £5 credit and an apology for having to defer payment on the previous arrangement.

Newly renovated, the Wavy Line stood out in a blotched and peeling concrete block of six purpose-built shops erected on the estate ten years earlier. A wool shop, tobacconist's and greengrocer's remained; two others had been boarded up. With its wavy blue-lined logo stencilled onto pristine windows, the Wavy Line spoke to the future. A confidence and ease not matched by Mr and Mrs Glynn who had poured more of their early-retirement money into the project than originally intended. It was rumoured that, as a young man, Mr Glynn had spent a couple of years at a university (before dropping out), and it went some way to explain the new ideas behind the Wavy Line, now reorganised with scientific precision. These days you entered through one door, were led through a one-way maze of aisles that ended at the cashier's counter, and exited from an entirely separate door. Retracing one's steps for a forgotten tin of luncheon meat brought tuts and sighs from Mr and Mrs Glynn but the limit of their patience was mostly exercised by the residents' refusal to understand that the centrepiece of the refurbishment, the revolving refrigerated display unit, was for display only and that items could not be extracted from it without mayhem ensuing.

I decided to linger a little outside, watching the cheesecakes circle, until it was nearly closing time. I filled up the basket slowly and methodically without enthusiasm and waited for the last customer to leave before approaching the counter. Mr Glynn carefully rang up the goods on the till; no sound cheered him more than the crunching buttons followed by the resounding ping. Each mark-up from the manufacturer's recommended price seemed to him a minor pools win and was registered on his face by a tiny explosion of joy that, in the six months since taking over the Wavy Line, had yet to desert him.

I was aware of Mrs Glynn, shuffling out of sight in the storeroom, running the broom over the same spot. I stretched up onto tiptoes and slid the note over the glass counter. Almost immediately the brushing stopped and Mrs Glynn emerged through a fine spray of dust, just in time to catch her husband removing his canvas Wavy Line cap and covering the note with it.

'Is that what I think it is?' There was a touch of exasperation in her voice, an affront not masked by the clearing of her throat.

Mr Glynn replaced the cap on his suddenly sad head. His lazy eye seemed to oscillate as he fixed the good one on me: 'Your mother is putting me in a very awkward position.'

'Why doesn't she ever come herself?' said his wife. 'Not fair on the boy. Getting him to do her dirty work. Not fair on you, is it, dear?' She looked to her husband for encouragement. 'It's not fair on us,' Mrs Glynn continued, 'not fair on the other customers.'

'Mrs Glynn is right, I'm afraid. Suppose everybody came in with their little notes. What then?'

'And it's not fair on your mother . . . to let things

get out of control.' Mrs Glynn ushered me towards the exit. The peal of the doorbell seemed to put a seal on the matter and I noted how Mrs Glynn signalled to her husband to begin turning off the lights as she pulled down the blinds on the door.

'What shall I tell my mother?'

Even in the early evening gloom I could see that Mrs Glynn brightened somewhat and she said cheerfully: 'Ask her to come and see us.'

'Ask her to come?'

'Perhaps tomorrow.'

I hadn't noticed the Mini at first when I emerged from the shop. But there it was, stationary and accusing. Bageye didn't look at me but just pushed open the door, and beckoned me in. If he'd observed anything of the business with Mr and Mrs Glynn, he wasn't saying. I sat and fiddled a little too long with the seat belt, so that he was compelled to reach over and close my door himself. He slapped the car into first gear.

We drove on in silence, passing our house along the way, as we headed towards town. I didn't like the manner with which he gripped the steering wheel or the exaggerated movements at each manoeuvre, or the overall bad energy in the car. I tried to push negative thoughts away but, now that I thought of it, wasn't it odd that he'd been waiting outside the Wavy Line? And hadn't he been too quick to say: 'Never mind. Dog must have gone with it'? I took a chance and asked him where we were heading, but Bageye wasn't saying a word, not one word.

The whole scene reminded me of something; it was elusive, like a half-remembered name, and then it suddenly came to me – those gangster movies where towards the end of the final reel, it was suggested to the hapless victim that perhaps he'd like to 'go for a ride'.

We stopped at the next set of traffic lights but when the lights turned green we still didn't move. There seemed to be some trouble with the gearbox. Bageye struggled to put it into first gear, then any gear at all. Eventually, he worked the gear stick so violently that it came off in his hand. Automatically, the bags swelled under his eyes.

Bageye turned off the engine, and told me to 'come out of the car, man'. He lowered his window and climbed out himself; leant back in and steered and pushed until he'd managed to roll the car round the corner onto a street bordered by a patch of wasteland. He applied the handbrake, picked up the severed gear stick, looked at it in disgust and disbelief, and suddenly threw it into the rough grass. You could see on Bageye's face that he immediately regretted it, though not enough to want to debase himself by retrieving the stick. With the crease of his handkerchief, he patted dry the perspiration that had begun to collect in his moustache and started walking. Without turning round he waved to me to follow him. We seemed to be going in the direction of Mrs Knight's.

Everything was 'as bad a sore' as my father used to say; surely it couldn't be worse. The car was kaput; he (or rather his son) had lost the bundle of ganja and some of the fellas had already probably paid up front for their share; the house money was only really loose change; and he was already a week late on his pardner money. On this last matter, Mrs Knight (via her humourless husband) would be bent on extracting the outstanding amount from Bageye before allowing him to sit in on the poker game. He would have to work something out.

It was just after 6 p.m. when we arrived at Mrs Knight's. In my mind I always spelt her name without a 'K' and always thought it a perfect match for her: she kept such strange hours and was mostly nocturnal. Mrs Knight was in her bedroom. We could tell because the bedroom light came on as we knocked at her front door.

The game wasn't supposed to start for another few hours; it wouldn't even warm up till midnight and Mrs Knight was obviously lying down for a little well-earned shut-eye before the proceedings began. We heard her whisper loudly: 'Who that now?' Her husband can't have budged, because she repeated herself with added emphasis: 'Who that now!' A few minutes later we saw the silhouette of Knight through the frosted glass in the front door coming down the stairs. He hesitated at the bottom of the stairs as if trying to identify the fidgety caller by his outline on the other side of the glass door and, having done so, was minded to wheel and mount the stairs to become familiar with a bed that, if he were quick enough, he might trick himself into thinking he had not yet left. But Bageye, who spied his host through the letter box, had dispensed with the knocker and was now banging on the door. When it opened he edged sheepishly past Knight into the hallway. 'Game start already?'

'Man, you don't know what time it is?' groaned Knight.

Bageye held out his wrist and laughed: 'Watch at the jeweller.' Since anyone could remember, my father's watch had been either awaiting repairs at the jeweller's or redemption from Bernard's pawnshop. It was never on his wrist. The man's concept of time was unique but made perfect sense to himself. 'Watch shoulda been fix from time,' he said apologetically.

Knight walked backwards out of the conversation like the surprised victim of a stick-up. He offered: 'Beer in the fridge.' He started back up the stairs, mumbling unconvincingly, 'Me soon come.'

I followed my father into one of the side rooms. Bageye examined the healthy collection of spirits in the dinky little bar that was modelled, like the one at our house, on the shape of the bow of a ship. He poured himself a tall whisky in a short glass. He broke off sooner than he'd wished as he heard Knight returning, and carefully screwed the cap back on the bottle. Knight came in, took the bottle from my father and gave the cap an extra twist before replacing it in the cabinet. 'Wha'appen, beer too good for oonno?'

'But, super, you wouldn't begrudge me a likkle drink.'

Knight gave him one of those 'Don't-mess-with-me' stares for which he was so famous.

'So you have that twenty for me' – Knight held out a hand to receive the pardner money owed to him – 'from last week?'

'Ten,' suggested my father. 'Hold ten for now.'

'Don't let me and you have argument,' said Knight.

Knight was a man you didn't ordinarily argue with. He was a man without charm. Charm was an alien concept, but if anyone could charm him, it was my

252

father. Bageye lifted his head and gestured that they should move towards the kitchen. 'Me have something for you,' he said solicitously.

Knight was his wife's junior by about fifteen years. He was her second husband – a saga boy, a zoot-suited sweet-back with, if the photos were to be believed, an adoring smile. These days the smile rarely came out. Back on the island, he'd been something of an amateur boxer: a full moustache hid the scar on a lip that had once been badly split; a front tooth had been knocked out and not replaced, so that he spoke self-consciously, like a cheap informant, out of the side of his mouth. Out of earshot the fellas named him 'Lazy Mouth' but in his presence you didn't joke with Knight. And you especially didn't fool around with Knight when it came to money.

He opened the fridge door, took out a plate of chicken wings and drumsticks; he selected a couple of pieces, and devoured them in no time, cleaning the flesh off the bone.

My father turned and waited for Knight to follow him into a back room. I was not invited to join them, and no matter how hard I strained, I only caught a smattering of the dialogue. 'All right, let's turn the argument,' my father kept on saying. Eventually their voices became hushed and conspiratorial. I heard Bageye suggesting a number of figures – 'ten to one' being the most pronounced and then that strange word 'accumulator'. Finally Knight's gruff voice softened, even though he'd begun to speak more loudly, and to my amazement, there were now guffaws coming from the interior.

Knight emerged first and mounted the stairs again.

Moments later my father came out from the back room. The gloom that had surrounded him earlier seemed to have evaporated. As we walked down the hallway towards the front door we heard giggling seeping out from under the door of the bedroom upstairs. And then the giggling stopped suddenly with the cold dry voice of Mrs Knight.

'But wait! You not even going to brush your teet'?'

I'm sure that Bageye had not fully worked out what he might do once we got there, but my father led the march back towards the Mini. I scuttled behind. Despite the drizzle my father didn't run. Bageye was not a man for running. Anyone passing would have seen a man seemingly buoyed by a private joke. We reached the car and he held open the passenger-side door like a skilled doorman of the finest hotel. He couldn't surely hope to drive the thing without a gear stick. No, but then he was Bageye, after all. On his very first try at turning the key the engine spluttered into life.

'You t'ink it can drive?' Bageye announced an attempt at the impossible: driving without a gear stick. It seemed as incredible to me as driving blindfolded. I could tell, as we say, that the idea 'sweet him'. In the years to come the fellas would still be arguing over it because, just imagine, as he did now, what the fellas would say when my father returned to Mrs Knight's that night. He'd strike a pose of unusual reticence and only then once their curiosity peaked, would he allow the story to be teased out, through their sceptical guffaws, only for them to have to take the shame once they trotted out to inspect the car driven – only Bageye would be mad enough to try – in such an amputated fashion.

It was beyond belief but there comes a time when a man has no choice but to recognise his own brilliance. Bageye chased the memory of when the idea had first come to him like the fork to the last pea on the plate. Now all that was required was a simple case of mirror, signal, manoeuvre. Mirror: Bageye pulled down the rear-view mirror to examine the smile and new laugh that would henceforth complement the slither of gold introduced recently between his right upper, outer incisor and canine. Ha, ha, ha. Signal: he pushed down the indicator switch. Manoeuvre: the engine whirred but the car did not pull forward. Though Bageye prided himself on his clutch control, the gears refused to bite. A cold thought stiffened somewhere between his cranium and frontal lobe that, having held out the promise, the kiss-me-arse car actually never had any intention of budging.

But there was not so much as one little curse. My father got out of the car and started walking. The unmistakable bounce in Bageye's step was the telltale sign. It could mean only one thing: we were headed for the bookies.

Jackass for Ride

THE ELECTRICITY MAN CAME TO empty the meter. We never knew what time to expect him. The nervousness about missing him meant that, though we were on our summer break and I'd been looking forward to a day at the rec, I was ordered to stay at home until he arrived. Everything about him was deliberate, even the way he wiped his feet on the mat, more times than was necessary. For such a fussy man, attentive to detail, it was odd that he never seemed to know who I was: I never failed to recognise him. The electricity man was slow and solemn as if charged with carrying out some burdensome task. He singled out a key from a bunch and unlocked the coin box from the meter. I followed him into the kitchen, watching him closely as he turned out the box of coins onto the table and began the count. He glanced back at me. He didn't want me looking over his shoulder but I'd been ordered by Bageye to 'mek sure the man don' skank you', and even though he was one of those dour old-timers who wouldn't have had the imagination to cheat anybody out of anything, I stayed nearby, just in case. When he'd finished, the electricity man pushed to one side those coins that he'd be leaving behind as the rebate and wrote out a little slip as proof.

There were few more pleasurable things than

counting and ordering the coins signed over by the gas man or electricity man, perhaps because it seemed as if we'd been given a gift or unexpectedly won something that couldn't have been hoped for. I piled up the coins, constructing miniature towers out of them and experimenting with varying the number of towers versus their height to see which arrangement looked more plentiful and likely to make a more pleasing impression on our father. It wasn't the biggest haul we'd ever had from the rebate but it was a pretty decent amount.

Bageye hardly bothered to look, never mind count the amount when he came home. He'd made the mental adjustment long ago between what we expected and what we'd end up with. He was just going to take enough for a packet of cigarettes, and leave the rest right there on the table for Blossom 'before she start her noise', he explained.

Word must have got out that things weren't looking too hot in the money department at Farley Hill because that same night we received a visit from Joe Burns. He'd been looking for a way back into my father's affections, it seemed to me, and that night he'd found it.

Joe had been somewhere up north making a delivery, and on his way back, with the empty lorry, he kept on passing farms with fields of sheep. Now, Joe Burns was the kind of man who couldn't keep evil in his heart. He'd been thinking about the war with Bageye and how it was ever going to end when an idea suddenly popped into his head that a farmer wouldn't miss one sheep. He pulled over, opened up the back of the lorry and kidnapped a sheep. Joe said the sheep's constant bleating reminded him of a friend he once had, so he called it Susan.

As soon as he reached Luton, instead of heading for his yard, Joe swung by ours at Castlecroft Road with Susan. Bageye acted as if it was normal for us to be delivered live sheep; he only had issues with the name. 'Susan' didn't work for him. That was more the name you might give to a pig. Had Joe thought of entertaining the name 'Mildred', he wondered. But Joe called out: 'Susan,' and the sheep looked up and that settled it. She was a damn good-looking sheep, he said and warned us not to get too attached to her because there was enough meat on Susan to last us the whole winter.

Joe Burns was the kind of fella that if you don't tell him 'no' straight away he took it as a 'yes'. And Bageye, not wanting to hurt his feelings, said he 'might can do something with the sheep'. He even offered Joe a few pounds but Joe said they were friends and friends didn't 'watch money'. He and Bageye tied Susan to the clothes-line pole in the garden. This was odd, especially when you considered how anxious Bageye was not to be talked about in the same breath as the smallees next door. He often complained that the Barkers were 'letting down the side, man' with their coop of chickens clucking through the night, allowing the Englishman to whisper about primitive darkies pretending to be civilised. But if all went to plan, Susan wouldn't be bound for very long because Bageye and Joe went out to find a man who knew a man who knew a butcher with some knives. Bageye returned alone but, when it came to it, he couldn't slaughter the sheep; and the following evening, before the night shift, he announced that he was going to set it free into the wild. He backed the Mini, working its new gear stick gently into reverse, to the entrance to the alley between our house and the Barkers', and somehow managed to bundle Susan into the car. He drove the short distance to the start of the bluebell woods and when he was sure no one was looking, opened the back doors and pushed out the reluctant sheep.

The next morning we woke to the strangely familiar sound of bleating and the sight of Susan coming up the road and stopping outside our house. Susan turned out to be one smart sheep. We hurried out to try to shoo her away but she slipped past us and trotted into the alleyway. Blossom got Milton to run to High Town to fetch Joe Burns with his lorry, and though Joe wasn't happy he took Susan away. At the end of the week Joe came back to the house with a huge bag of frozen meat, and this time he accepted the few pounds Bageye offered him, as Blossom muttered under her breath: 'If you want jackass for ride, here comes Bageye.'

She pointed out to Bageye – what he might have forgotten – that we had no freezer and our fridge wasn't big enough for all the meat. Bageye simply shrugged as if the dice had rolled badly for him or he'd been given a poor hand at the poker table: 'If it go so, so it go.' Though Blossom cooked mutton soup and curry for the next few days, we could hardly bear to eat. Every time we raised a spoon or fork we thought of Susan.

The fast-approaching school term had not been mentioned for some time but, although nothing was said, it seemed to be the main topic. It was a bit like the phoney times when we pretended things were normal though really they were not; like when a window would have been broken and you hoped Bageye wouldn't discover it but equally couldn't bear the tension of it not being discovered. The atmosphere was as charged and heavy as the air before a thunderstorm. But if our father was even more irritable of late then it was probably because he had swallowed his pride to beg the foreman for all the overtime going. Though he overslept, he was not getting enough shut-eye.

He bought an alarm clock – one of those with a round face and copper ears for bells – and spent a scary amount of time setting it precisely to what he imagined was two minutes past the hour he'd need to rise. It always sprung to life ahead of itself. He wound it tighter, as if it had wilfully gone off early; tightening it so that it'd hold to the allotted time. It never did. The next evening Bageye wound the clock with even more force and was nonetheless surprised when the spring snapped. He brought the broken clock downstairs, searching our faces for evidence of sabotage. Somehow, someone must have weakened the springs because springs were made to be wound, right? Right? He could find no confessors but wondered aloud in a dry voice whether we agreed with him that he didn't need an alarm clock anyway because he had a house of helpful pickney that 'never stop make noise'. He slammed the clock down on the dining table. He looked over to the TV and thought about ripping the plug from the lead again but obviously decided it wasn't necessary, or that he was fed up with having to do it. He turned and climbed the stairs back to his bed. Bageye left behind a vacuum. It was filled with silence.

There were never any volunteers to wake Bageye. You had to be shamed into doing it, like going to confession on Saturday morning. There was a rota of sorts but no one could ever agree whose turn it was. You couldn't count on the rumour that someone had volunteered as that was probably just a ruse so that you'd relax. The time would creep up on you as you slid into the mental quicksand of children's TV. But even as you watched you never fully let go of that sense of dread. Until, with one eye still glued to the monitor, you'd begin to draw yourself away from *The Pink Panther Show* show or *Bonanza*; pull yourself up and out of the force field that was sucking you into the very TV itself. For there was a danger that you'd look up and find that everyone but you and some other fool had slunk off, the way the jungle animals in the movies suddenly disappeared ahead of some unexpected catastrophe, an army of locusts or a forest fire. At that juncture the last two left behind could not hope to escape without some sort of commotion that would have disturbed the dying moments of Bageye's sleep. You'd be trapped with each other.

Milton might have looked as though he was dozing off on the settee but really he was primed as always. He was ready. It was wise to be ready too. On your marks. I slipped my feet into my sandals. Get set. Every fibre of my calf muscles twitched. And two minutes before the hour, maybe even five minutes. Go! I rocketed out of the settee, out the door, out

261

ahead of the pack, well before Bageye woke with bloodshot eyes.

My father had not raised the subject of the missing package since our visit to the woods. In any event, it was our secret. But not a day had passed without me kneeling by the bed and renewing my pact with God for the return of the package in exchange for lifelong devotion. It never really occurred to me that it would amount to anything. Kneeling and praying was just something you were supposed to do, like putting on your school uniform before going to school or brushing your teeth at night. It had to be done right, of course. Sometimes, I went along to confession and was so bothered about the absence of sins, scribbled on a piece of paper the night before, that I made up a few more on the spot for Father Gerry kneeling on the other side of the wooden grille. Though the punishment of ten Hail Marys and suchlike was a bit of a chore I loved the idea of absolution and especially the words: 'Go and sin no more.'

In the dream you rise from your bed and stumble towards the bathroom just in time to relieve yourself. You wake from the dream and are surprised by the stickiness of your inner thighs and the dampness of the sheet underneath. Well, that's just how it was now. My feet had taken me for a walk (I had nothing to do with it) and mysteriously I found myself in the woods at the very spot where we thought we'd buried and lost the package. As I'd wandered from the house, I'd been dreamily thinking what a miracle it would be, how it would make everything right again, if only God would intervene and lead me to the missing package. Now, as I looked down at my feet, there it was. It was a little bruised, and some of the brown paper had been nibbled at by insects or a small animal, but otherwise it was intact. At that moment, I should not have been surprised had the clouds parted and the sun come out to a heavenly chorus. I was the third child, after all, and the third child is always blessed.

I brushed off the dirt from the paper, made sure there were no creepy-crawlies lurking anywhere, lifted my jumper, breathed in and found room for the parcel under the waistband of my trousers. The package might split at any moment. Inhaling and holding my breath for thirty seconds at a time, I made it to the edge of the woods. There was no one about and only one vehicle to pass, a big white van, parked at the side of the rec, before I reached the house. My luck held. The van was empty, or so it seemed. For a second – no, more – I thought I heard whispering but there was no driver or passenger in the cabin, and you couldn't see into the back because the windows on the side of the van were mirrored. As I drew closer the whispering appeared to stop, or it might have been that I had imagined it all along. I should have kept going but the windows drew me to them: I couldn't resist checking my appearance in the mirror, to see whether I looked as suspicious as I felt. And an odd thought occurred to me, the memory of what the fellas had said that time at Mrs Knight's: 'Is Bageye son, dat for true.'

My nervousness now was that the van was sure to have disappeared by the time I got back and told the others. They would have been just as thrilled as me.

Occasionally, you'd see vehicles about with tinted windows but mirrored ones were a first.

I quickly dropped the idea when I entered the dining room because I had clearly got my timings all wrong. There was still an hour to go before we needed to wake Bageye. *Bonanza* was still running. As usual Horse was removing his ten-gallon hat, wiping the sweat from his brow and putting Little Joe straight on some matter. I announced a little too forcefully, I suppose, that it was my turn to wake Bageye. Everyone was flummoxed and a little suspicious of my sudden enthusiasm to volunteer.

'Let's get this straight,' said Selma, twisting a kink of hair through her fingers. 'You want to wake him?'

'Uh-huh.'

You had to be super smart with Selma. She had a way of pretending to be irritated or simply uninterested when really she was extremely interested. I decided to change the subject and tell everyone about the van. If they went up to the front bedroom and craned their necks through the window they'd just about be able to see it parked beside the rec. They all, apart from Selma, traipsed out.

'What are you hiding?' Selma asked.

I ignored her and, crouching in front of the TV, attempted to adjust the volume knob. 'Ah ah ah.' Selma warned me off fiddling. *Bonanza* was coming to an end anyway, she said. In our house, deciding which programme to watch was matched only in its intensity of feeling by the correct level for the volume. It seemed to take hours of negotiation before we settled, as we always did, on one or two notches above silence so as not to disturb Bageye. Even a skilled lip-reader would have had trouble working out what was being said. But you didn't mess with the volume, unless of course you were nervous about something else and had forgotten the rules.

'You're shaking. Why are you shaking?' Selma asked. 'And you smell.'

'You smell too.'

'No, no, you really do pong,' she continued. 'What is that smell? Like a wet dog.'

I pulled the jumper more tightly over the package. Selma wasn't likely to give up now. If I stood up she'd ask what was under my jumper, so I started making my way to the door, walking crab-like on my haunches. Milton almost knocked me over coming back in.

He was out of breath and excited. 'There's something going on outside.'

'You see it, then?' I asked, straightening up casually.

'See what?' Milton gave me one of his famous exaggerated looks. They were designed to annoy me.

'What's wrong with you?'

'A ewe is a female sheep,' Milton answered.

'The white van?'

'Yeah?'

'You see the windows?'

'It's not that difficult, is it, dummy?'

'How d'you mean?'

'I mean, it's parked outside our house.'

'No, it's not.'

'You wanta bet?'

Milton was enjoying himself too much for it not to be true but I decided on taking a look anyway. Before I'd even reached the hallway he and Selma pushed on and climbed the stairs – still mindful of making too much noise – ahead of me. Milton wasn't lying. The van was parked outside our house. Although there was still no one in the cabin, strange intermittent sounds, like a series of radios being tuned, were now coming from the back of the van. I wasn't surprised when Mum also turned up in the bedroom and pushed to the front, mumbling to herself: 'The Devil is a bad man.' I had a queer sensation of having seen all this before, somewhere, somehow. Some other time I'd watched them press their noses to the windowpane in her bedroom and wait for something, anything, to come out of a white van. I'd climbed the stairs to the bedroom that I'd already climbed, following them, along a path and sequence of events that I'd already witnessed. So I wasn't surprised, not really, when after a period of intense staring at the van, its back doors swung open and men in police uniforms jumped out.

'My bad eye a-dance,' Mum's voice cut through the anguished groans from us children at the sight of the half a dozen or more policemen, some carrying garden forks and shovels as they emerged from the back of the van. 'I see trouble in this house tonight,' cried Mum. A hand – it might have been hers – squeezed on my arm. We pressed to her side and, as the policemen strode towards our house, moved as a block back from the window.

The walkie-talkies blared outside our front door, then the angry knocks and the banging began. 'My bad eye a-dance,' Mum was wailing now. 'Judgement! Judgement!' She let go of me and her arms began to flap, rhythmically but also as if they were beyond her control. The banging continued. Selma whispered that

I should go and wake Bageye. I suddenly wasn't so keen. She persisted. 'You have to. Somebody has to. Before they break down the door.'

Selma pushed me out of the bedroom and onto the landing. I crept over to the spare room where Bageye slept and put my ear to the door. His breathing was heavy and rasping but despite the banging he was still asleep. I tiptoed in. A blanket was pulled tightly up over his head. But for the breathing it could have been a mummy from an Egyptian tomb in that bed. I prodded with one finger through the blanket. Bageye didn't move. That far-off, uncaring, unconcerned dreamland still held him. To wake was to break the spell, to begin that prison sentence of family life, the unforgiving grind of factory work and debt and more debt. Bageye slept, man. Sleep was his friend; wakefulness was the enemy. I prodded him again and when that didn't work, I had no choice but to shake him. He stirred and I backed towards the door. He pulled back the covers and I immediately saw the enormity of my mistake: his eyes were on fire.

'Who dat?'

'It's wake-up time,' I answered.

'Time already?' Bageye reached over for the clock. 'But what the rass,' he growled. 'It not even six. What dat noise?'

'Someone at the door,' I answered. 'Some men at the door.'

'So answer it nah!'

Whatever I said next was critical. It had to be judged right, so that Bageye might get some idea of the gravity of the situation. 'It's some white men,' I explained. The package was beginning to irritate my skin, as if it was forcing me to do the right thing and tell my father. But the Devil is a bad man. When Satan tempts you, and introduces an idea, and you accept it, then you are in his grip. I wanted to be able to explain to my father – but it was not the right time – that if something's lost, a package for instance, might it not be lost for a reason? The Devil helps you find it when maybe it would be best left alone. It wasn't my fault: it was the Devil's work.

The banging was so hard now that the front door rattled. Bageye wheezed and spluttered, rising up from the bed. He swung his feet out and perched on the side, giving himself time for the cough to work its way round and somehow out of his chest. His arms and legs looked pitifully stiff and heavy. He eased himself into his work clothes, carefully as you might do if you'd broken or fractured a limb. My father pointed towards the dressing table and I fetched the tobacco tin for him. He measured out the amount for a smoke, and rolled a thin, tight cigarette, just enough to get him going for the night – just a starter. The knocking and banging persisted but there was no way Bageye was going to hurry now, especially not for white men. He took a match from the box. Though I didn't like the smoke it was always a pleasure to watch how elegantly he struck the match and waved it out after use. Only when he'd finished the last draw on the cigarette did he head for the landing.

The others had already made their way to the hallway, and when they saw Bageye descending the stairs they made a pretence of trying to open the door in a confusion of locks, catches and bolts. They paused and parted for him as he reached the final stair.

We left our father there and retreated to the kitchen where Mum was still wailing and foretelling the doom that was nearly upon us. We sheltered behind the plastic strip of curtain as Bageye worked through the combination of locks and bolts to free the vibrating door. A tight scrum of policemen filled the frame of the doorway. It was odd how they appeared more nervous than Bageye. I suspect it was because they were excited. Our father may have been a little awkward but really you imagined him as a host who had been caught slightly off guard by the unexpected early arrival of guests.

'Clinton Grant?' asked the policeman who looked the most senior of the bunch.

'Mr Grant,' answered Bageye.

'Mr Grant, we're here to search your house.' The police officer had one of those nasal voices that sounded as though it was full of cold but was actually full of disgust.

'You have a warrant, man?' asked Bageye.

The policeman turned his shoulder towards Bageye and tapped on the three stripes of his jacket. 'Sergeant! Do you have a warrant, sergeant? OK?'

'OK, captain,' said Bageye. 'Me never mean anything by it.'

The sergeant nodded and produced a piece of paper. Bageye studied it and, still reading, invited them in. 'Mek sure you wipe your feet.'

Two men remained outside with fork and shovel, and went to work on the garden, digging it up. The three or four others shuffled in. They were giants in big boots, clumsy and poorly coordinated like adolescent schoolboys not yet used to their size. The sergeant said they'd start upstairs and Bageye answered that he was not hiding anything.

'Is that right, sonny?' asked the segeant.

Bageye bristled. For a moment he failed to understand that the questioner was not addressing him but staring through the striped curtain at me. While his men were upstairs, the sergeant started to search the living room. Bageye marched into the kitchen and called out for Blossom but she was pacing up and down in the garden, calling out to God. My father rounded on me. He didn't have time for any foolishness. I must tell him now what the sergeant meant. 'Wha'gwan?' he whispered. 'What did dat man mean?'

I was unable, physically unable, to speak. Eventually, I slowly lifted up my jumper. The package bulged up and though Bageye recognised it instantly, he half exclaimed: 'But what is this? What is this? Lawd, give me strength.'

For the first time that night Bageye looked worried. He tried to pull out the package but it was stuck, and I was unwilling, despite his command, to undo my trousers in front of him. Together we managed eventually to ease the package out. We could hear the sergeant leaving the living room and coming down the hallway. He was only steps away and Bageye spun round, just in time clasping the package behind his back.

As Bageye stood stiffly talking to the sergeant, answering his list of questions, Selma came up and stood behind him. If he was unnerved by her presence it didn't show, and without flinching he accepted what was going on behind his back: Selma tugged at the parcel till he released his grip. And in the same action, she turned, lifted her skirt and somehow wedged the package underneath. Selma winked at the rest of us and walked casually into the dining room and sat in front of the TV.

When the clumsy policemen had finished upstairs they started on the downstairs. They were rough with everything. The drop-down door which had survived all this time like a loose, rotten tooth finally fell free from the hinges. The sergeant apologised. He also said he was sorry about the grille to the air vent that had been pulled out and couldn't be restored to its rightful position. He even tried a joke about his men being breakers not makers. But the joke stopped when, having been through the entire house, they still hadn't found what they were looking for.

'We're going to have to search you, Mr Grant.' A steeliness had entered the sergeant's voice. Bageye said he was happy to oblige but then he wanted them out of his house. He held out his arms and spread his legs, and one of the policemen patted him down. There was nothing to be found.

'And the children, Mr Grant. We have to search the children.'

'No, no, no,' Bageye pleaded. 'You don't have to do that.'

'Why not?'

'You don't have to do that.'

'Why not? You give me one reason why not, Mr Grant.'

'Give me a minute,' said Bageye softly.

The sergeant looked as though he wasn't going to budge. There was a parade-ground stiffness in his bearing but he couldn't fully keep it up. 'I must be going soft,' he said. And taking a deep breath, he added: 'You have exactly one minute.' He rounded up the other officers and ushered them to the front door.

Immediately, Bageye pulled the dining-room door open and asked simply: 'Who have it? Give it to me.' For a moment Selma remained stubbornly holding out. Bageye asked again, and she half turned in the chair to protect her modesty, slipped the package from under her skirt and handed it over.

Amidst all the hullabaloo, there was a strange calmness about Bageye. He came over to Selma and for the first time anyone could remember, placed a hand gently on her shoulder. He told me to stop my noise even before I had time to summon the tears that were all too ready, telling me to remember it was not my fault. He went to the back door. Mum was still pacing but calmer now, soothed by the hymns she had started to sing. Bageye stuck his head out the door and shouted to her: 'When you don't see me, I gone.' Finally he walked into the hallway. There was some indistinct murmuring before the front door was opened. The last words we heard before they took him away was Bageye saying: 'You can tell your men that them can stop digging now.'

The Devil is a Bad Man

BAGEYE NEVER WENT TO JAIL. We only found out when, one day, Mr Barker's son stopped me outside the house and told me: 'Your father is a bad man.' He said it with no particular malice, merely as a statement of fact. He had the proof, he said, right there in his hand. The boy held up a copy of the *Luton News* already open on one of the middle pages. In one long column there was an account of the raid, the arrest and trial, and a little passport-sized photo of Bageye.

'Your father is a very bad man,' he repeated. I didn't bother to tell the Barker boy that he was wrong; that it was the Devil who was a bad man; that it wasn't my father's fault; that he was a man like this – 'If you want jackass for ride, here comes Bageye'; that he was a noble and foolish man who would take the blame for something even when it wasn't his fault.

We never knew that the court case had come up. Mum never spoke about it. At the trial, the judge handed down a stiff fine: several hundred pounds, an amount equivalent to two years' wages from Vauxhall Motors. If the fine went unpaid then he would have to spend time at Her Majesty's pleasure at a local prison. In the end, the fellas clubbed together (Mrs Knight is even said to have contributed); the money was found and the fine was paid.

The raid seemed to have made up Mum's mind. She was convinced now that her husband would always 'tek chance' and she didn't want to live that way any more. She had tried it his way, and it didn't work. She would take charge from now on. Her first move was to take out an injunction against Bageye (citing examples of cruelty towards her and her children) and the court ruled that he was to be barred from the house, in fact barred from coming within a mile of the house on risk of further prosecution and possible imprisonment.

After a while we stopped listening out for signs of Bageye; for the welcome click of the front door closing as he left, the angry yanking of the toilet chain or scraping of furniture across the floor.

On 4 September 1972, we rose early. Milton and I cleaned behind our ears with a wash rag, put on our expensive school uniforms and squeaky, polished brogues, and, clasping (more like swinging) our leather briefcases, entered the grounds of St Columba's College. Somehow our mother had managed to scrape together the funds to send me and my brother to private school. And I dare say, it was an achievement that Bageye would have been proud of.

We heard that Bageye had moved in temporarily with Joe Burns. Months later we received a visit from Joe at Farley Hill. He came with a big, unguarded smile, and was laden with boiled sweets and two more bags of corn on the cob. Mum was grateful for them.

Towards the end of his stay Joe announced that he had one more important task to perform before he went away. He made Blossom promise that she would hear him out. We gathered in the living room to hear

Joe confess that the truth was he'd been sent by Bageye. The sweets were from our father and the corn also. And Joe said that we had to believe him, and say as much before he'd continue.

He had a message from our father. Bageye was sorry for all that had transpired. Things had gone hard for him. He had accepted that. In true form, he had taken it on the chin and moved on. But he'd also realised, said Joe, that he was nothing, less than a man without Blossom and the children. When the time came to meet his Maker, he didn't want to be lowered into the ground with no one mourning him. Bageye wanted to come back to the family. Would we take him back? Could we find it in our hearts to welcome him once more into the fold?

On several occasions as Joe spoke, Blossom tried to intervene. She was minded to run him, no matter the gifts, from her yard for being Satan's messenger. But Joe held up his hand each time and placated her. She would have her say but his spar, Bageye, wanted to hear what the children had to say first.

The strain showed on Joe's face: he looked exhausted. In fact, we were all spent. There was a lull in the conversation, deep and unsettling. It went on for so long, we thought it would never end. Finally Selma took it upon herself to gather us children for a separate conference in the dining room.

Joe slumped in a chair in the living room for the next half-hour, listening attentively to Mum's litany of Bageye's misdemeanours.

'Him can change,' said Joe. 'In fact, him already change. You t'ink him gwan let a little gambling split up the family?'

Mum kissed her teeth: 'Him cyann' change. Is pure brand new second-hand.'

She said it repeatedly in answer to any point Joe tried to make in our father's favour, giving space to the individual words 'brand – new – second – hand'. She said it so often, you realised it had been rehearsed; that she had steeled herself to say it over weeks, perhaps even over the years, and was frightened lest she lose her resolve. They both stopped the argument when we came back in and Joe stood to attention.

'Well?' he asked.

'We couldn't agree,' answered Selma, 'so we took a vote.'

'So, do you want your daddy back?' asked Joe. 'Or not?'

No one spoke. Joe said that we didn't have to answer straight away. We could take our time. He also wanted us to know that our daddy would be ringing any minute now. It was odd to hear the word 'daddy' as none of us ever referred to Bageye that way; even acknowledging the word now felt like some kind of betrayal. Moments later, just as Joe had promised, the phone rang. The cream plastic phone had only been acquired recently and took pride of place in the hallway on a specially designed table-and-seat combination made of wrought iron. Selma walked determinedly to the hallway.

'Luton 55182,' she answered, holding the phone away from her ear just as sophisticated ladies did in the movies. We could hear our father's voice coming back down through the earpiece but apart from repeating the newly memorised telephone number, Selma said nothing else; Bageye's tiny voice, trying not to, sounded increasingly irritated. Selma pulled the phone even further from her ear. She looked as if she regretted not wearing gloves, and after a minute of staring at it, even though Bageye was still speaking, Selma replaced the receiver.

'Wrong number,' she explained when Joe looked at her wide-eyed and expectant.

Immediately, the phone rang again. It sounded urgent, even furious. When it was clear that no one would answer, Joe picked up the receiver. He nodded slowly and respectfully, as if Bageye was standing right there beside him. 'Let me ask,' said Joe into the phone. He covered the mouthpiece with his hand. His eyes sought mine. Joe waved the receiver at me, beckoning me forward, and thrust the phone into my hand.

Bageye was on the line. 'Is my little spar, dat?'

He called my name but despite willing myself to say something, anything, no words came. My jaw ached the way it sometimes did when I concentrated on a new task.

'Is my little spar, dat? I can hear you breathing.' Bageye spoke softly. He had something to tell me. He wanted to know whether I would listen. I nodded and it was as if he could see me.

'Remember when you was up in the hospital that time?' asked Bageye. 'You might not remember. You musta been two, maybe three. Well you was in the hospital for a month, and every day when me finish work me come look for you. Every single day. When I reach now . . .' Bageye's voice trembled. He paused for a long while. Eventually, he cleared his throat and continued. 'Me see you there a-stand 'pon the bed waiting, waiting you know. And you know what the nurse them did tell me? You wouldn't let not a one of dem touch you or change your dressing, apart from your father. You remember? You cyann forget dem kinda t'ing, my frien'.'

Minutes must have passed before I realised Bageye had stopped talking. It was only when Joe peeled my fingers from the receiver that I was aware I'd been gripping it so hard my hand ached. Joe kept his eyes on me all the time. He readied himself to speak to Bageye into the mouthpiece.

'Listen, old man,' said Joe, 'you better stay where you is for now.'

Joe put down the phone. He summoned a brave smile that failed fully to arrive, and walked slowly to the front door. Moments later we heard the engine start and he was gone.

In the months that followed, on at least two or three occasions, I thought I spied Bageye behind the wheel of the Mini on the outskirts of Farley Hill. But before I could be sure the car always sped off. If any of the others had also seen him then no one owned up to it.

We settled into life without our father. The seasons changed. Christmas came and went. There were no more imagined sightings of Bageye, and I no longer found myself, strangely, passing by the betting shop or lingering outside of Mrs Knight's, pretending to remove an empty can from the hedge.

Acknowledgements

I thank my parents and all of my siblings for their generosity in allowing me to tell this version of the story.

Early drafts were improved by Jo Alderson and our children, Jasmine, Maya and Toby. I am especially indebted to Jo for her wisdom and clear eye, and for introducing me to new thoughts about retrieving and intervening in the past.

Bageye at the Wheel began as a short story and as a calling card to my charming agent, Kevin Conroy Scott. I'm glad that it brought us together and is now, several years later than intended, realised in print.

Enormous credit is due to the wise Ellah Allfrey who spotted Bageye's potential early on and hurried him into the pages of *Granta* magazine.

Dan Franklin has shown great care and attention in bringing the book to life. I was encouraged hugely in the writing by Dan, and Tom Avery's enthusiasm.

My thanks also to Viv Adams, Nicholas Rankin, Robert Donald, Fiona Durdy, Chris Jablonski, Julia Arrow-Smith, Snežana Ćurčić, Emma Dyer, Michael Rosen, Dan Shepherd, Harriett Gilbert, Eka Morgan, Jay Mukoro and Sajida Perween, who all spent many hours reasoning with me on the merits of the *Bageye* stories down the years.

I am grateful to Richard and Hilary Alderson, and Sam Stringle, for lending me their homes to enable me to finish the book.

Hats off to Sophie Lambert and colleagues at Tibor Jones. And all respect to Chloë Johnson-Hill, Steven Messer and the team at Jonathan Cape who have acted as midwives to *Bageye at the Wheel*.